Humanism and Behaviorism in Physical Education

by
Robert E. Gensemer

National Education Association
Washington, D.C.

Note
The opinions expressed in this publication should not be construed as representing the policy or position of the National Education Association. Materials published as part of the NEA *Aspects of Learning* series are intended to be discussion documents for teachers who are concerned with specialized interests of the profession.

Acknowledgment
Excerpt from "Emotional Arousal and Motor Performance" by Joseph B. Oxendine in *Quest* (January 1970), p. 29, is reprinted with permission of the author and the National Association for Physical Education in Higher Education.

Library of Congress Cataloging in Publication Data

Gensemer, Robert E
  Humanism and behaviorism in physical education.

  (NEA aspects of learning)
  Bibliography: p.
  1. Physical education and training—Study and teaching. 2. Humanistic psychology. 3. Behaviorism (Psychology) I. Title. II. Series: National Education Association of the United States. NEA aspects of learning.
  GV363.G46   613.7'07   79-25368
  ISBN 0-8106-1488-X

Contents

The Author

Robert E. Gensemer is Associate Professor of Physical Education and Director of Graduate Studies, Department of Physical Education and Sport Sciences, University of Denver.

The Consultants

The following educators have reviewed the manuscript and provided helpful comments and suggestions:

Richard C. Burnham, Physical Education Specialist, Seattle Public Schools

Bobbye Whitworth Selbo, Physical Education teacher, Heritage High School, Littleton, Colorado

Dr. Herman Weinberg, Chairperson, Professional Physical Education Department, University of South Florida, Tampa

CHAPTER 1

Will the Real Method Please Stand Up?

It's likely that we all have one prevalent, emphatic, and genuine factor in common: We want to be successful teachers.

But just exactly how do we do it?

It isn't easy, but neither is it as difficult as we are too often led to believe it is. This is not to say that teaching is, or ever will be, a simple matter. Or predictable. Or easily managed. Or artless. Quite clearly it's just the opposite. Teaching is an endeavor which requires, for success, the greatest amount of preparation, spontaneity, ingenuity, and technique. In practice it becomes both art and science—the art of awakening the curiosity of students and the science of satisfying such curiosity. Teaching affects the future welfare and the lives of human beings and is thus a responsibility not to be taken lightly. Possibly, it's the most challenging of professions.

Encouragingly, the instructional methods now available are the most effective in the history of education. Today it is much more possible to be realistically and legitimately successful than ever before. Best of all is the fact that the available techniques are supremely logical and direct, with no secrets or complexities. Everything is straightforward.

Virtually every contemporary teaching format has its stimulus in one of two predominating systems—one a collection of philosophies generally referred to as HUMANISM, and the other a science-based technique called BEHAVIORISM. Together these systems have influenced educational thought more than any previous methodological approach. Consequently, it can be accurately said that

ALL ACCEPTED PRESENT-DAY TEACHING METHODS ARE AN EXEMPLIFICA-TION (OR A VARIATION) OF EITHER HUMANISM OR BEHAVIORISM.

Each of these systems consists of a set of associated ideas organized around a foundational concept which serves as a guide for teaching. Each believes that all significant teaching is a functional variation of its basic method. Because both humanism and behaviorism contain a great deal of logic, it is possible to listen to one side and then the other and to be convinced of the value of both, at the same time being confused as to which system is better. Both make good sense. The positive feature of both systems is that their greatest attention has been given not to trying to convince or confuse, but to making the teaching process more effective for teachers and more enjoyable for learners.

Being Lost and Being Found

Because of the many recent changes in educational methods and technology, it's easy to be confused today. All the philosophy, theory, and research which have become available so rapidly can make a good deal of sense, however, if they are mixed into some usable form for the classroom. Consequently, the task of assessing and comparing the quantities of information has been one of the principal ventures of modern education.

Physical education has had its own particular influx of new information. The speed in accumlating ideas and knowledge seems to have doubled, tripled—increased a hundredfold—in recent years. Not so very long ago, teaching physical education was far less complicated. Now, however, it may include guided discovery teaching, competency-based instruction, behavioral objectives, systems analysis, movement exploration, gaming and simulation, cybernetics, transactional analysis, biofeedback, visual motor behavioral reversal, supraconsciousness, and other topics.

These developments need not be so confusing if we view them as positive responses to a changing world and a changing educational scene. Furthermore, we need not feel that all our new endeavors also require drastically different teaching methods. And therein lies the real value of humanism and behaviorism. When we understand the principles of these two systems, we find that they provide a readily adaptable approach which allows us to take any direction we wish with our teaching. These systems are not so much concerned with *what* a teacher wants to do as with *how* it may be done. It is not necessary to cloud our thinking with a multitude of methods, because humansim and behaviorism are essentially the only two techniques needed. Thus we can give our attention to such matters as deciding on objectives.

It's very similar to Vince Lombardi's comment about football teams: "Extraordinary teams do not do extraordinary things; they do ordinary things extraordinarily well." So it is with teaching: Excellent teachers do not do outlandish, exotic, or mysterious things; rather, they do very straightforward things. Humanism and behaviorism are not outlandish, exotic, or mysterious techniques; they are, as teaching should be, very straightforward.

This book offers an analysis, an application, and a combined arrangement of both systems, particularly as they relate to the teaching of physical education. The attempt is to make the composition of humanism and behaviorism as pragmatic as possible, with an overall objective of assisting teachers in their endeavors to make teaching and learning more efficient, effective, and rewarding.

Before we can proceed, however, it is first necessary to establish the understanding of a very critical element which is an absolute requirement for successful teaching, no matter which method or combination of methods is used. It is a condition of organization, a *prerequisite* to any method. Without it, teaching is merely a random occurrence.

CHAPTER 2

A First Essential

Effective teaching demands purpose. All successful teachers, and indeed successful people in any venture, share a common characteristic. Often, this quality is referred to as *orderliness*.

This means that success is related to responsible, goal-oriented behavior. Teaching must be performed with intention and resolution, manifested through clear and definite objectives, with well-formulated plans for achieving those objectives. In other words, one cannot expect to be successful without some sort of organization.

This does not mean being narrowly confined to any set of externally imposed means and ends. Orderliness does *not* demand particular objectives or methods. Individual teachers can have individual objectives and can employ individual techniques for attaining their objectives. Orderliness does require, however, that objectives and methods be present. We must know where we are going and how we are going to get there.

Without question, then,

FOR TEACHING TO BE SUCCESSFUL, ORDERLINESS IS AN ABSOLUTE.

And more directly:

ORDERLINESS MEANS HAVING DEFINITE OBJECTIVES AND AN ORGANIZED PLAN FOR REACHING THOSE OBJECTIVES.

In the art and science of teaching (ignoring for the moment any personality factors which may influence success), orderliness exists as the most useful tool available to a teacher. In fact, orderliness and success are so closely related that one can be said to be predictive of the other (Travers 1973). Moreover, orderliness is even *more* important than method since its first requirement is to establish clearly defined objectives, and the very act of doing this, as we shall see later, will automatically determine the appropriate method(s) to be used.

A Certainty Among Uncertainties

This emphasis on orderliness may sound fairly presumptuous, particularly since the teaching/learning phenomenon is probably one of the most difficult of all human enterprises to investigate, to understand, and consequently to make conclusive statements about. In reality, if the writings of recognized authorities are assembled and analyzed, the inescapable conclusion is that there is simply no agreed-upon overall formula for guaranteed success in teaching (MacDonald and Tanabe 1973) for *all* teachers, for *all* settings, at *all* times.

There is, of course, no shortage of research and observation on the teaching process. What emerges from the many studies is in fact not a complete prescription for instant success, however, but a list of factors which appear to be related to success. Apparently there are certain factors which by themselves cannot assure the teacher of effectiveness, but when they are a part of the teacher's behavior, they provide increased *potential* and *probability* for success. And the one factor which consistently shows up as the most common feature of success is that of orderliness.

Admittedly, the idea of "success" in teaching is itself quite a variable, subject to great differences in definition. What one researcher may have considered success another may not even have thought about. How success is determined, however, is completely immaterial; for within the wide range of different existing definitions, orderliness still manages to rank as the most critical ingredient in whatever definition of success is accepted (Gage 1963; Broudy and Palmer 1965; Raths, Pancella, and Van Ness 1971; Travers 1973; Lortie 1975; Bennett 1976; Merrill and Tennyson 1977; Pullias 1977; Hammill and Bartel 1978; Tschudin 1978).

Orderliness in Reality

Orderliness is a rather strange word. Like all words, sometimes it helps to know what it does *not* mean. It should therefore be clearly understood that orderliness does not imply that the successful teacher needs to be businesslike to the point of using autocratic control, granting students little freedom for decision making. Rather, orderliness means the tendency of the teacher to be systematic and methodical in both self- and class management. In practice, such management can occur in classes which are relatively unstructured, where students are allowed a great deal of opportunity for individualistic and self-directed behaviors. In fact, there can be an almost total lack of teacher intervention with those students who are making self-initiated progress in a setting which is completely open. Underneath it all, however, in the situations that work, there will always be found a purpose and a regulation to the classes, no matter how subtle they may be. In some cases, the atmosphere may be one of complete student freedom. In others, there may be considerable regularity. But in all successful settings, the teacher involved always has cognitive organization and responsible, goal-directed class environments.

The Foundation of All Things

It's not so surprising to find orderliness as the main component of success. In a global perspective, order is a very commonplace thing. It exists in everything that has managed to survive the test of time—numbers, language, clocks, architecture, music, football, traffic lights, one-way streets. All of life itself seems to have an invariable organization. In the natural world bird fits with branch, deer with meadow, and stone with soil. This concord has been worked out over millenniums.

Order may also be evident in places which at first appear to lack structure. For example, the free play of children, which appears to be without any arrangement at all, has its own peculiar conformations. Its structure has been the subject of considerable research (see especially Wade 1976). Theorists have contended that the internal formats of play can shape and focus lifetime behavior (Denzin 1976), or that certain psychic and social adult preparedness is learned through free play (Kleiber 1976), and that acceptable play behaviors can be and possibly should be taught to children (Ellis 1973; Wolfgang 1976).

It also appears that there are people who do not lead organized lives and who are still successful. In particular, creative people are assumed to be disorganized, without any plans, their ideas coming not from prede- termined precision, but from some mysterious dark corner of their minds in complete spontaneity. The source of their creativity cannot be explained simply as erratic mind-wanderings, however. Nor is it a product of black coffee, or a few glasses of wine, or drug highs, or mystical trances. Instead, it comes from logical, analytical, and reality-oriented brain functioning. Creative people simply use their thinking processes differently from non- creative people. Although they may engage in a great deal of abstract thought, eventually their reasoning is channeled into logical, orderly, and strategic deliberations (Martindale 1975).

Orderliness Is Not Every Teacher's Virtue

If everything that is successful and all things that have survived through time have organization, why, then, should there be some teachers who do not have it? Indeed, there is good evidence to indicate that dis- organized behavior may possibly be the most prevalent factor in teacher failures (Smith 1975).

Surely, this absence of organization cannot be explained by a lack of research studies or available writings on the teaching process, for there are many of these. Instead, it must come from other sources. In a survey of thirty American colleges, Erickson (1975) found that less than half of the graduates in physical education felt "very well prepared" for their first year of teaching, and a mere fourteen percent said that the teaching methods courses they took in college were "very helpful" in preparing them for their profession. This is a particularly critical finding since it appears that the college student of today is perhaps more concerned with gaining effective professional career preparation than students have ever been before (Rice and Cramer 1977); it may also explain why more than half of those students who enter college with the intent of preparing for teaching have changed their minds by their senior year (Astin 1977).

On further analysis, directionless teacher behavior may be caused by the prevailing atmosphere in many of today's schools. If the setting is disarranged, it is difficult to be organized in a situation which fights it.

Another possible explanation may be that educational information has outdone itself; that is, we know too much. By expanding our knowledge we may have also increased our confusion. The hazard of a knowledge explosion is that our attention is drawn in so many divergent ways that it becomes difficult to find direct solutions to specific circumstances. Or the real meaning of an issue may become so cluttered with details that the rationale never appears. Two main considerations result from this situation: (1) it is a positive condition—because so much information is available, it is possible to see many solutions to any specific situation; and (2) the direct solution (which will be discussed later) is to analyze the nature of the objective in a specific situation, and in doing so conclusive answers relative to appropriate procedures may be found.

Method Cannot Exist Without Orderliness

Given the commitment to orderliness, then, only two major questions need to be asked relative to method: (1) What educational outcomes do you want for your students? and (2) What educational experiences will achieve these outcomes? The first question is essentially personal, to be answered by each teacher on an individual basis of what is most important. The second question is the basis of this book.

CHAPTER 3

One Fence; Two Sides

During the late nineteenth and early twentieth centuries, Europe underwent a cultural revolution—one still too close to us in time to be grasped in full. It doesn't even have a name, except for the vague term *Modernism*. Most importantly, it ultimately set off a tremendous revolution in educational thinking and stimuluated the still-existing debate between humanism and behaviorism.

Some very well known people were active during this period—Max Planck, Bertrand Russell, William James, Picasso, John Watson, Pavlov, Einstein, Freud. Together they stirred the world into some deep philosophical thinking and managed to give human beings some long overdue self-respect. The outcome was a realization that all individuals were—individualistic.

Jean Jacques Rousseau had realized this a hundred and fifty years earlier, but when he wrote about his ideas on individualizing education, he was thrown out of his native France. Then, when John Dewey made his educational theories known during the early twentieth century, everyone seemed to remember what Rousseau had said. Dewey spoke about "learning by doing"; Rousseau had believed in something called "naturalistic" education. Doing what comes naturally, they seemed to say. This basic concept gathered a growing number of educational revolutionists who strongly encouraged a free-school and open-classroom environment which fostered the idea that teachers should offer only minimal mediation in the lives of students. The design, which came to be loosely known as "progressive education," was a revolt against the highly disciplined educational process common at the time. Essentially, it held that students should be allowed to direct their own learning in a "natural" manner, as they saw their own needs. Not only should students determine *what* they should learn, but also *how* and *when* they should learn it.

The cultural revolution which stimulated individualism and progressive education also awakened the world to the importance of science. Consequently, in academic circles, there was a rather widespread feeling that education should take on the same format as other sciences. Proponents of this concept believed that a scientific methodology was the only

11

way to assure that learning would occur. Therefore they encouraged an instructional technology often referred to as the "Science of Education," which featured a stronger belief than ever in traditional education—favoring teacher authority, teacher-directed instruction, correct responses from students, and a structured curriculum.

Despite distinct differences, these two factions greatly influenced American education in the twentieth century. For a while it appeared that the scientific approach would completely take over, particularly following World War II when the growth of educational technology and research, and increasing specialization forced school curricula into concerns which were strictly academic. During the 1960's, however, the United States experienced the emergence of a youth-oriented counterculture. Vietnam was a critical issue, religion floundered, family bonds weakened, and other symptoms of confusion and moral drift appeared. Resultingly, much attention was given to the effect of education on American society. Many persons who saw education as the great salvation of the country believed it was failing in this endeavor. Thus, antiauthoritarian forces, such as the Students for a Democratic Society (SDS), arose, and the educational literature became saturated with writings which called for radical school reforms. The effect of these tremors was to produce the greatest philosophical and technological self-evaluation that education has ever experienced. And the results are still being felt.

Today, although the arguments of progressivism and traditionalism are old hat, nonetheless they are still alive and influential. They exist in their updated versions of humanism and behaviorism. The fundamental beliefs of these two systems are distinct, particular, and generally opposed to each other. Both have considerable value. Both are realistic. Together they are the most critical concerns education has ever encountered.

Physical education has also been caught up in the humanism/behaviorism debate. This is a very practical issue, and to a great extent the future directions of the field will depend on how the two sides are harmonized. Fortunately, there *is* room for both systems, and there *is* a way for physical education to employ the best elements of both in a combined teaching arrangement. But before we discuss this arrangement, let us examine more closely the foundational concepts of both humanism and behaviorism.

Student Independence or Teacher Regulation

The most fundamental disagreement betwen these two descriptive models of the teaching/learning process lies in their assignment of the responsibility for learning. Humanism says that students are quite capable of, and therefore responsible for, their own learning. In contrast, behaviorism states that teachers are more competent in stimulating learning and are consequently answerable for the process. Thus, the exact difference:

HUMANISM ASSIGNS THE RESPONSIBILITY FOR LEARNING TO THE STUDENT, WHILE BEHAVIORISM ASSIGNS THE RESPONSIBILITY FOR LEARNING TO THE TEACHER.

12

Humanism exists today as the major nonprogrammed teaching format in education. Specifically placing emphasis on the self-directed activity of students, its concern is with such factors as creativity and self-discovery. Thus it proposes that education should be very personal and characterized by an attention to human interests. Supporters of these concepts have understandably become known as humanists.

HUMANISTS ARE CONCERNED WITH THE INTERESTS AND IDEALS OF PEOPLE.

The behaviorist model of teaching, on the other hand, is representative of a branch of psychology which relies on a stimulus-response view of education. Consisting of a set of concepts which have arisen from the application of behavioral technology to the interactions of teachers and learners, it includes in its framework the theory from the programmed instruction movement of the 1960s. Proponents of this psychology are appropriately referred to as behaviorists.

BEHAVIORISTS PLACE NO EMPHASIS ON THE CONCEPT OF THE HUMAN MIND BUT ARE CONCERNED INSTEAD WITH THE OBSERVABLE BEHAVIORS OF PEOPLE.

A casual observation can only lead to the conclusion that a very irreconcilable difference exists between these two philosophies of learning. On the one hand, the behaviorists contend that humans are very lawful—that is, they respond in predictable ways to specific environmental situations. Given a set of circumstances, they say, the reaction of people is foretold. Therefore, to produce a particular behavior, all that is necessary is to organize the environment into the conditions which are known to provide the particular behavioral result. This is the old idea of reflexes, now called conditioned responses; the design is the product of laboratory research which began with rats in mazes, pigeons in boxes, and dogs who were hungry. The countless hours of watching these animals react to changing stimuli brought researchers to the conclusion that human behavior is subject to natural laws similar to those which operate in the zoological world. Consequently, behaviorists claim that people are very predictable and therefore controllable.

Not so, say the humanists who believe that people are predictable only in that they are unpredictable. The only thing you can really predict about people is that you can't predict what they will do. Human beings do not respond in classical ways to classical situations, and in no way do they respond to the same laws which influence the behaviors of rats, pigeons, and dogs. People are too philosophical and thus will react differently—individually—to the same environmental setting.

In a very general analysis therefore, a major difference in the two viewpoints is that

BEHAVIORISTS BELIEVE THAT PEOPLE ARE PREDICTABLE IN THEIR BEHAVIOR, WHEREAS HUMANISTS CONTEND THAT PEOPLE ARE INDIVIDUAL AND UNPREDICTABLE.

13

Behaviorists believe in the simple idea of stimulus-response—S–R. Basically, a given stimulus will produce a given response. Therefore, knowing the stimulus, one can predict the result, say the behaviorists.

The humanists make an important addition to this formula. Between the stimulus and the response they place an "O" for the organism, the human being—S–O–R. The organism is a thinking, feeling, value-oriented human being, interpreting the environment in unique ways and responding individually in accordance with each person's interests, evaluations, and experiences. According to the humanists, responses are not determined by one's simply being *in* the environment, but by one's appraisal of the environment.

Behaviorists can foresee human perfectability as a result of their science. By explaining all behavior in terms of its causes or conditions and by knowing the controls of behavior, they believe it becomes possible to accelerate all human processes, including learning. In a sense, behaviorism is an approach to the long struggle toward human perfection.

Humanists see this procedure as undemocratic and amoral. Such an attempt at control leaves less to be credited to people themselves. Humans are spontaneous and original, with the capacity to choose and to be held responsible for their choices. They are free to express themselves as persons, as evidenced in such endeavors as art, music, literature, and sport. Unlike rats or pigeons or dogs, human beings can, indeed *must*, resist any effort at being completely controlled.

Both humanism and behaviorism have a rightful place in any educational setting, for, basically, both are usable. Blind adherence to only one philosophy as a teaching guide is only a half-truth; it is far more reasonable to use aspects of both. Collectively they can combine to make the teaching process more effective than either one alone; and, as we shall see, both can be used by the same teacher, with the same students, in the same setting. If nothing else, the very positive factor evident in both systems is that they are aimed at producing success.

To fully understand how these two theoretical constructs can fit directly and particularly into the teaching of physical education, it is now appropriate to take an even more careful inventory of each one separately. A more complete understanding of the basics and versatility of each system is essential before we can effectively appreciate their values. Then we can make rational interpretations and generalizations from the two systems and apply them to our own teaching.

The Humanistic System

Humanism proposes the fundamental concept that all people are in command of their own destinies. Each person is aware of individual emotions; each is a sum of characteristics and qualities which set the individual apart from all other persons. All attitudes, feelings, and values are personal to each individual. Best of all, humanism contends that people are inherently, intrinsically, and constitutionally good. Every individual is therefore deserving of dignity and of the well-stated "inalienable right to life, liberty, and the pursuit of happiness." Thus, since people are the makers of their own futures, and since they are virtuous by nature, the best form of education is a free and democratic organization, for only in such an atmosphere will students realize their full potential.

Therefore:

HUMANISM IS A WAY OF THOUGHT AND LIFE WHICH TAKES AS ITS MAIN CONCERN THE REALIZATION OF THE TOTALITY OF ALL HUMAN RESOURCES.

As it relates to education, humanism starts with the assumption that teaching is a relationship between *human beings* which involves *human behavior, human meanings, human understandings,* and unique *human experiences.* The feelings and perceptions of teacher and students are every bit as important as knowledge. In keeping with this philosophy, a humanistic educational setting is one which seeks to enrich and enoble the lives of students by liberating the full potentialities of their every resource.

Separate Meanings and Nonmeanings

Despite its widespread application, humanism remains today an often ambiguous and misused word. It may therefore be helpful to recognize that humanism does *not* have any connection with religion; neither does it have the same implications as the words "humanitarian" and "humane"; nor does it have a relation to the academic study of the humanities. Even in educational circles the word is often applied in many ways, including affective education, psychological education, open classrooms, free schools. Nevertheless, in spite of sometimes erroneous or confusing applications of the concept, certain characteristics of the philosophy appear to be constant. They are the central doctrines which define the very spirit of humanism. As applied to education, they are as follows:

1. The idea of *human potential* reappears consistently in humanistic education. Learners are seen to possess a great potential of *positive abilities;* consequently, teaching focuses on the development of these abilities. Moreover, humanism grants students a fully conscious and free will, with the potential for each student to recognize positive individual abilities. Humanism, then, is a very *positive* approach to education as it focuses on the personal *potential* of each student.

2. The most prevalent cluster of positive human abilities that concern humanists are those considered *human relations*—those abilities which help people to get along with others. Accordingly, education should accent the social lives of students with a learning atmosphere which encourages everyone to be genuine with the self and others. Such an atmosphere allows each student to be open and honest, without fear of reprisal, and requires that the teacher be largely *nonjudgmental* about the feelings and opinions of students.

15

3. Perhaps the most important aspect of humanistic education is the recognition of the *affective domain* and of the critical role of the schools in its development. Education of the affective domain involves the cultivation of emotions—an education for "feeling"—just as cognitive education is aimed at intellectual growth It starts with a teacher who is capable of being a sensitive, warm, emotional person "turned on" by many things; one who is able to relate enthusiastically to students. Its major objective is development of self-awareness and insight which will result in an increased interest in such creative endeavors as originality, imagination, and novel interpretation, with the final product a general positive feeling about learning. When it accomplishes its aim, affective education replaces any "I-feel-stupid" or "I-hate-school" attitudes with positive self-images and a sincere intrigue with learning. Thus the ultimate objective of affective education is to assist people in becoming caught up in the sheer joy of living. Of all the humanistic endeavors, this is probably the most difficult to accomplish. According to the humanists, however, it is also the most neglected dimension of formal education. The schools, they contend, are too much involved with the cognitive aspects of learning and should be providing a more total education in what might be described as life enrichment.

4. To accomplish the foregoing objectives, it is necessary that the teacher be a *facilitator* of learning, which is markedly different from being an "imposer" of learning. Humanistic education moves away from teacher-controlled classes to shift the determination for learning to students. Consequently, the teacher must be more supportive than critical, more understanding than judgmental, and more accepting than demanding. Since students are given full credit for their ability to make choices and evaluate their own progress, the curriculum should therefore focus on the concerns and interests of students rather than on those of the teacher or the school system.

Getting Beyond the Words Is Difficult

Describing the central objectives of humanism is difficult because the words used are often idealistic and visionary and are prone to misinterpretation largely because of their freehanded implications. In addition, although other descriptive words are available, they are too restrictive for use with some humanistic concepts. This is especially true when narration of the humanistic experience falls into the realm of existentialism. As a concept, existentialism itself is extremely difficult to describe. In its most undiluted sense, it means to "become." More specifically, it means that students become "aware"—not as we normally become aware of the world in an intellectual manner, which is a sort of *object* awareness. Existentialistic learning is more of a *subject* awareness—a *method* of realization; learning to know things in and of the world, with a "knowing" and a "seeing" that incorporate the dimensions of time, relativity, causality, and morality. Accordingly, humanistic education should promote self-

16

fulfillment. What this means, directly, is that each student should realize her/his own positive human potential, become well acquainted with the self, as it were, and reach full functioning in art, music, sport—in all activities.

Abraham Maslow (1970) may have said it best when he called it *self-actualization*, which is now a widely used term. Maslow meant it to refer to a sort of exploitation of individual talents, capacities, and potentialities—an actualizing, or making real, of one's own abilities. In physical education, this can directly mean the cultivation of one's physical potential, or it can more indirectly mean experiencing one's expressive self through a motor medium.

Castles in the Air

Unfortunately, say the humanists, education is so engrossed with intellectual affairs that it never gets around to these existential and self-actualizing experiences. Too much time is spent on external matters and too little given the inner person. The emphasis is certainly on external achievements, specifically attaining high grades. Even in physical education, with its great potential for self-actualization, concerns all too often center on who can run the fastest, or do the most pull-ups, or win some sort of championship.

Moreover, the humanists condemn society itself for its emphasis on external concerns: obtaining the highest-paying job; buying a better television, an extra car, a second house; taking a more expensive vacation. Eric Fromm (1964) said that most people are "necrophilous"—attracted to the mechanical aspects of life. In contrast, some persons are "biophilous"—infatuated with life itself. Necrophilous persons are attracted to things that are not alive and, in some cases, are even against life. They like to talk of money, gadgets, and machines. They prefer memory to understanding, having to being. They approach life mechanically, liking things they can possess and disliking uncertainty. In counterpoint are the biophilous people, who have a love of life itself. They have the quality of existence one describes as "full of life." Attracted to the *process* of life, with an aptitude for wondering, biophilous people have an ability to see the "whole" of living, to examine all things, and to grow by stimulation rather than by force. For such persons, good is all that is conducive to growth, and evil is all that strangles life.

Obviously, then, humanists believe contemporary education and technological society are both caught up in a syndrome which supports necrophilous attention. Worst of all, they say most people don't even know it and consequently don't know what they're missing. Fortunately, however, humanists also believe the situation is not hopeless.

The Preparation for and Restoration of Life

Historically and philosophically, education has always been considered some variable form of "preparation for life." The years of formal schooling are intended to provide people with the equipment necessary for an effective existence in society. Accordingly, education is often thought to be a reflection and creator of society. The schools are therefore in a position to *change* society. In fact, humanists believe that education *must* change society. It is their firm conviction that education is the most logical place to implement the ideals of individual worth and self-actualization. Thus:

HUMANISM PLACES ITS GREATEST FAITH FOR A SANE WORLD ON THE POTENTIAL OF EDUCATION FOR GENERATING INDIVIDUALS WHO WILL HAVE THE CAPACITY TO LIVE SELF-FULFILLING LIVES.

Education reaches all people, it is relatively autonomous, and it has already demonstrated its ability to change the values of society. It is a powerful force, one that—more than any other—can turn people to the more meaningful concerns of their inner selves. Best of all, humanism incorporates physical education as an integral and extremely important part of this potential.

But to accomplish all these ends, traditionalistic teaching must be discarded and new methods utilized wholesale. Humanistic teaching is never a matter of "telling" things to students; instead it is made up of moments when teacher and student reach some insight into the nature of things and of beings. It is more an inspirational teaching, with credit for psychological respectability given teachers, and a capacity for self-discovered learnings accorded students. The themes of this biophilous and somewhat existential experience include freedom, trust, and discovery. Most certainly it is self-centered—not in the sense of conceit, but of self-actualization. In the most exciting meaning of the word, it is an education for being *alive*.

Self-Appropriated Learning

The most prevalent characteristic of a humanistic educational system is the confidence it places in self-discovered learnings. The valued outcomes—those concerns which are self-actualizing, biophilous, and existential—are matters which are meaningful to each student in an individual and personal way. As such they cannot really be communicated from one person to another in a traditional teacher/learner fashion. The teacher cannot merely declare their existence, explain their function, and impose them on students in the same manner that factual information can be tutored. Instead, these inner learnings are matters which each student must discover individually, without the pressure of specific time requirements. Therefore, rather than using static techniques teachers must create an environment which stimulates student discoveries of natural things through individual initiative. To accomplish this end, an attitude of freedom is necessary to allow teachers to conduct classes in an atmosphere of open permission for student self-discoveries—a replacement for the rote memorization and restricted thinking often found in traditional education.

The critical elements of the implementation of the humanistic approach to education, then, are as follows:

HUMANISTIC EDUCATION IS FOUNDED ON THE CONCEPT THAT THE ONLY MEANINGFUL LEARNINGS ARE SELF-DISCOVERED.

Correspondingly, the basic humanistic belief is that all persons are capable of directing their own affairs. Consequently:

HUMANISTIC EDUCATION GIVES STUDENTS THE RESPONSIBILITY FOR THEIR OWN LEARNING.

Therefore:

THE EDUCATIONAL ATMOSPHERE MUST BE ONE WHICH STIMULATES SELF-APPROPRIATED LEARNINGS.

Overall, such a discovery-type system of education proposes a different sequence for learning. In a traditional approach the principles for solving problems are presented first, and the various instances of their application are given second. Facts are learned first and the value of the facts is learned second—a standard two-stage method. In discovery learning, however, students are asked to solve problems without first having the solutions. The teacher does not tell students the principles or generalizations (or facts) they are to learn, but instead involves them in a process of exploration, leading them to self-discovered conclusions by presenting an arranged set of problems, with cues given when necessary. Thus, humanistic education proposes a reversal of the traditional system.

IN A DISCOVERY APPROACH TO LEARNING THE INSTANCES (PROBLEMS) ARE PRESENTED FIRST AND THE PRINCIPLES (SOLUTIONS) SECOND.

Discovery-type learning is, by its own arrangement, self-appropriated rather than imposed on students. The process involves analysis, logic, and synthesis in a self-governing operation, and the result is not only the knowledge obtained, but also a refinement in the learning capacity itself. The psychological activities involved in problem-solving are enhancing by themselves, for students are said to develop "organizational abilities" from their experiences. What is acquired is not only the discoveries, but also an *ability* to make other discoveries.

IN DISCOVERY LEARNING IT IS NOT ONLY *WHAT* AN INDIVIDUAL IS LEARNING THAT IS IMPORTANT, BUT ALSO *HOW* IT IS BEING LEARNED.

Learning accomplished through discovery is believed to constitute a particularly influential and meaningful kind of knowing. The real product is a more comprehensively perceptive person. The knowledge gained is the result of abilities unique to each student; it is therefore more personal, more meaningful, and more transferable to other situations.

19

Physical Education Has Been Moved

Physical education has listened intently to these developments in recent times and has now taken an important role in the discovery format with a broad and sometimes misunderstood theme. *Movement education* has achieved a remarkable acceptance in the profession, particularly as it applies to the elementary school curriculum. Its philosophy includes all the precepts of humanistic education; its method is one of self-discovery. Therefore it can be concluded that

MOVEMENT EDUCATION IS PHYSICAL EDUCATION'S METHODOLOGICAL ANSWER TO THE HUMANISTS.

Movement education gives a freedom for expression and a sanction for creativity to students, and it relies on experimentation and problem-solving as its principal methods. It fashions originality, organizational ability, self-reliance, self-discovery, self-fulfillment, and all the other humanistic values. In a very real sense, it is a freedom for expression through a motor medium—self-actualization through physical movement, or biophilic physical education, if you will.

The values inherent in a humanistic approach to physical education are the same as, and the ends identical to, the values and ends that humanists propose for general education. Only the *means* are different. And that difference may be the greatest benefit of all, for in using a physical medium to promote the aims of humanistic education the resulting development of self-actualizing properties also incorporates the relative mastery of general movement and the potential refinement of specific mastery of general movement and the potential refinement of specific motor skills—an extra dividend which only physical education can offer in a total school curriculum.

Logical, sensible, reasonable? But wait—there's another side to the story.

The Behavioristic System

On the other side of the proverbial fence are the behaviorists, who find humanism far too philosophical and speculative. They argue that discovery learning is very difficult to support with the sophisticated kinds of research familiar to behaviorism; and they express serious doubt that humanistic learning can ever be as effective, meaningful, and lasting as claimed. Besides, even if its claims were true, it is much too time-consuming, and legitimate education cannot afford to stand around and wait for the results. Furthermore, the process of discovery itself contains too great a frequency of error, hence it is much too inefficient.

The behavioristic system of education is fundamentally stimulus-response teaching; that is, in its simplest version the teacher asks or presents a problem (stimulus) and the students answer or solve the problem (response). The method is unadulterated and direct; its effectiveness is fully supported by research evidence.

The foundation of behaviorism is very clear: the manipulation of the environmental conditions to which a person is exposed will bring about definite and predictable behavioral results. Depending on how the environment is manipulated, it is possible to produce behaviors that never existed before, to maintain existing behaviors, or to eliminate behaviors. The underlying theory is that behavior is preceded by *causes*. Everything that people do is a product of the environmental conditions which existed just prior to their behavioral responses. Each behavior is a *result* of the events that occur prior to the behavior. Therefore:

PEOPLE RESPOND TO THE ENVIRONMENT (OTHER PEOPLE, SITUATIONS, AND EVENTS) IN VERY PREDICTABLE WAYS.

Consequently:

BY CONTROLLING THE ENVIRONMENT, IT IS POSSIBLE TO INFLUENCE HUMAN BEHAVIOR.

In education, the behaviorism model operates on the conviction that teaching can maximally influence learning by controlling the conditions of the environment. Very directly, it is a means of managing teaching to produce efficiency, with the methodological procedure based on objectivity, precision, and economy. The final result is the implementation of intentional and predictable changes in the behavior of students.

It's Classical and It's Mod

There it is—change in behavior—the end effect of using behavioristic psychology. This objective also results in much criticism of behaviorism. Strangely enough, however, behavioral change is also the most frequently stated dictionary definition of learning.

On this ground, at least, all educational theorists must agree in principle with behaviorism. The intent of education is to produce learning, which is a change in behavior. The behaviorists simply claim to know how best to do it. In contemporary literature, they speak of the technique as "modifying" behavior; subsequently their strategy has come to be known as *behavior modification*.

It doesn't really sound too bad—behavior modification. But many people still don't like it. They see it as pure control, and link it with such things as dominance, regulation, restraint, autocracy, dictatorship—all of which seem amoral. In truth, however, these criticisms are unjustified. Behaviorism *does* mean control, but it does *not* mean to curb, restrain, or hold back students through an authoritarian dominance. Rather, it means to maximally arrange the environmental conditions for positive influences on learning. It is a matter of educational management which, although it does include a relative degree of control, is not aimed at dominance but at making the educational enterprise more effective.

It's the Here and the Now

Behavior modification is one of the most influential doctrines ever to penetrate education. It has generated more writing and research than any other teaching strategy in the history of education (Roberts 1975). If for no other reason than its very magnitude, it has also produced an inordinate number of critiques.

The essential endeavor of behavior modification is to influence people to perform precisely defined responses. Always, the end product is a specified behavior; thus the success (or failure) of the methodology can be clearly seen. For example, a mother may want her six-year-old daughter to make her bed every morning or a fourth grade teacher may want a student to be able to recognize all the states of America. In both cases, the behavioral objectives can be easily stated and observed, and are not achieved until the bed is made daily or the fifty states are identified. If a high school physical education teacher wanted a student to swim ten lengths of a pool using a side stroke, then that behavioral objective is not accomplished until the student swims the ten lengths with a side stroke.

It's all very clear, very well defined, and very observable. The goal is precisely stated and is not achieved until it is actually observed. In this important respect, behaviorism differs markedly from humanism.

BEHAVIORISM STATES ITS OBJECTIVES IN VERY PRECISE TERMINOLOGY; AS A RESULT, THE RELATIVE SUCCESS OF TEACHING CAN BE EASILY OBSERVED.

The important factor is clarity. The more clearly stated the objectives, the more easily understood they will be for teachers and students alike, and the more error-free the evaluation of their achievement.

Making the Subjective Objective

Of course it is often difficult to state objectives in precise terms. Some are so broad in concept that they almost defy any description. For example, physical education frequently lists such standard objectives as "cooperation with others," or "an appreciation for the game," or "an awareness of strategy," or other subjective goals. For behaviorism, such purposes are too vague and nonmeasurable and must be replaced by more precisely defined objectives for the specific behavioral responses to be expected of students.

To satisfy this concern, the initial emphasis in behavioristic education is *not* teaching, but the description of *definite objectives*. Consequently the essential task of teaching then becomes one of influencing students to perform the necessary functions which will result in the accomplishment of these objectives. From the behaviorists' viewpoint, historically education has been relatively ineffective because it has not defined its purposes in precise behavioral specifications. Such concepts as "understanding," "appreciation," and "awareness" may be legitimate educational objectives but are unacceptable to behaviorists until they are precisely defined in terms of what students must do to demonstrate that they *do* understand, they *do* appreciate, and they *are* aware.

It becomes difficult at times. For instance, an art teacher may state an objective for an art class to "develop an appreciation of good art," which sounds like a perfectly logical expectation. But exactly how does one develop such an appreciation? Moreover, exactly what is the criterion for good art? Most importantly, what behaviors will demonstrate that a student does indeed have this appreciation? Can it be shown simply by a developed interest in paintings? Or by the ability to recognize the works of known artists? Or by doing one's own artwork? Or by agreeing with the teacher on what constitutes good art?

Obviously, there are problems. What may generally be accepted by the humanists as noble and logical objectives are quite unacceptable to the behaviorists. In the opinion of behaviorists, humanism is invalid because of its philosophical values. How can biophilous objectives be defined? How can a student demonstrate self-actualization? And as for existentialism, even an attempt at scientific explanation is a corruption of the concept itself.

The point remains, however, that validity is possible only when the objective being considered can also be exactly described. For educational goals to be valid, according to behaviorism, they must be stated in precise and accurate language. This is a very difficult but critical concern which will be discussed in greater detail later in this book.

Programming the Instruction

When educational objectives have been carefully defined and the desired student behaviors precisely delineated, behaviorism next demands that the educational process itself be exactly outlined. The progressive steps to be required of students must now be constructed. It is a matter of determining how best to arrange the educational environment for maximum learning to take place—that is, deciding on which student experiences will best accomplish the task of meeting the stated objectives. These experiences, too, must be carefully defined and the educational conditions organized into an arrangement of tasks of increasing difficulty, with students progressing from one step to the next only after mastering the previous step.

This deliberately structured series of educational tasks arranged in order of increasing complexity is often called programmed instruction. Its first application came through the use of teaching machines specifically designed to present programmed material to students. Such a machine gives the student an incomplete statement or a mathematical problem through a "window" arrangement that withholds the information or answer until the student responds. Then, the correct response is shown, and the machine next presents a problem of increased difficulty. This format has also been used in textbooks. Normally, the reader covers an answer with a card until the question has been read and answered, then checks the accuracy of the response, and proceeds to the next question.

Computers have now taken over where the teaching machines and programmed textbooks left off. Although their ability to interact with human learners is of course limited, computers can reproduce some surprisingly complex teacherlike situations, and they have been shown to be an amazingly powerful and highly efficient instructional tool (Glaser and Cooley 1973). The major element in computer instruction, as in teaching machines and programmed textbooks, is how well the program itself is designed. This, too, is the main task for the teacher using a behavioristic format.

In this version of education, teaching is not primarily a stimulus to learning; rather it is an arrangement of the conditions which will *expedite* learning. Thus the effectiveness of behavioristic teaching depends on the skillful production of the learning program itself. Therefore:

> THE RELATIVE SUCCESS (OR FAILURE) OF A BEHAVIORISTIC APPROACH TO EDUCATION IS DETERMINED BY THE EFFECTIVE ARRANGEMENT OF THE LEARNING ENVIRONMENT TO PROVIDE THE PROGRESSIVE STEPS WHICH WILL LEAD TO THE ACHIEVEMENT OF THE PRECISELY STATED OBJECTIVES.

This does not say that students can learn without a teacher. What is emphasized is the structure of the learning tasks. In this context, teachers are most effective when they act as "engineers" instead of companions to students. Successful teaching thus becomes a matter of how well the teacher can design and administer a systematical "program" of instruction rather than how inspirational one may be.

It's Not Who You Are, But What You Do

Behavioristic education seems to give its attention to the precise designing of instructional programs with little concern for the act of teaching itself. One may easily conclude that teaching is subordinated to and somehow less than the design of the instructional program. Indeed, this is a rather perplexing characteristic of behavioristic philosophy. Behaviorists do not deny that the personality of the teacher is important, however. All they are really saying is that the character and personal idiosyncrasies of the teacher are simply less *dependable* in promoting educational efficiency than those factors which can be more dependably designed.

Furthermore, the analysis of what constitutes effective education is made by observing *students*, not teachers. When students show that they are learning prescribed material through a specifically designed programmed instructional arrangement, the problem of teaching is largely solved. It's all in the method. The distinctive description of objectives and the precise organization of the steps to attain them constitute not only *what* it is that is to be taught, but also *how* to teach it. Teaching in a behavioristic scheme is therefore mostly a matter of managing and programming the overt behaviors of students.

Incompatible Inferences

Should it, then, be humanism or behaviorism? One philosophy says that flexibility and adaptability are the teacher virtues, while the other says teachers must adhere to carefully planned programs. One side says teach students, and the other says teach subject matter. One says promote individuality, and the other says produce predetermined skills. One seems to say freedom, the other control.

Both sides *do* appear to exist in a realm of apparent truths, and each seems to be founded on indisputable fact and/or theory. Unfortunately, however, the proponents of each format have often become obsessed with convincing others of their value and in the process have overconfirmed their own opinions within their own viewpoint. Further, both sides have missed some of the substance of their philosophies which, when appraised, is actually an agreement between the two.

It seems that a sensible midpoint of synthesis is yet to emerge. What needs to be done, then, is to combine the two sides into a reasonable and usable package. The value of the two approaches to education does not lie in the absolute acceptance of only one, but in the consolidation of the best elements of both. Even more logically, instead of a sort of middle-of-the-road compliance, there is instead an apparent situational point which moves between the two, for there are times when the teacher needs to be openly humanistic in the educational environment, and other times when the setting must be behavioristically controlled, even with the same students. The effective teacher is therefore one who, rather than holding strictly to the doctrines of either side, is able to apply both formats, in varying degrees, as the situation warrants. Without question:

EDUCATION CAN READIY UTILIZE THE COMPONENTS OF BOTH HUMANISM AND BEHAVIORISM; AND THE PERCEPTIVE TEACHER IS ONE WHO RECOGNIZES WHEN TO USE COMPONENTS OF EACH METHOD

Productive teaching is a matter of timing the use of each method. The intriguing thing is that physical education, as we shall see later, by the very nature of its subject material has a built-in and direct way of telling the teacher when to use humanistic attitudes and when to rely on behavioristic techniques.

On Stage, Where It All Gets Serious

The discussion so far has provided a theoretical and philosophical perspective of humanism and behaviorism. It is now appropriate to step outside the conjectural confines and envision how each system can be used in an educational setting.

Four examples follow. Each is hypothetical, although a random sampling of any sizable school district would probably turn up situations similar to those presented here. The first two examples are third grade classrooms—one with an open, humanistic atmosphere, the other with a behavioristic format. The next two illustrations are of high school golf classes—one taught with humanistic discovery-type techniques, the other utilizing behavioristic principles. These examples are probably extremes—that is, the teachers involved are showing relatively strict adherence to one of the two teaching strategies, and it is not likely that very many teachers are so singular in their method at all times. Nonetheless, these examples are presented in this fashion to illustrate the possibility of approaching the same educational setting in two entirely different and distinctive ways.

A Humanistic Third Grade Classroom

It's difficult to tell when you first enter this room what sort of organization it has, if any. The room is arranged into "centers" of particular themes. One corner contains books to serve all curricular needs, along with recreational reading material and books specifically designed to help children improve their reading skills. Another area is a viewing center with filmstrips, slides, viewmasters, and stereoscopic viewers. A listening center contains records and tapes, with earphones so that users will not disturb the rest of the class. There are also an art center, a science center, and a math center, each with appropriate educational material for children to explore freely; as well as a cooking area, a construction area, and a discovery table which contains piles of what might otherwise be considered "junk." A very noticeable feature of the room is the lack of traditional rows of student desks. In fact, there seems to be an insufficient number of desks for all students to use simultaneously.

Students in this classroom are dispersed into small groups which they have spontaneously formed in keeping with their particular interests at the moment. They change groups and centers frequently. A teacher and a teacher's aide move around the room, dividing their time into small, concentrated periods with the groups. Each gives attention as stimulator, adviser, consultant, and resource person, rather than giver of knowledge. Each listens and watches a great deal and talks less than a traditional teacher.

At this particular moment, the teacher is with a group at the science center, while the aide is sitting on the floor with other students. The rest of the class is clustered in groups at the various centers, working independently of any teacher attention.

At the science center students and teacher are watching sand filter through an hourglass. The conversation goes something like this:

TEACHER: Why does it do that?

MICHELE: Why does it do what?

TEACHER: Why does the sand in the hourglass flow downward?

DAVID: 'Cause there's a hole in the thing.

(Some muffled laughter occurs.)

TEACHER: No, no, I mean, why does it go down instead of up?

(Silence)

The sand has now filtered through the hourglass. The teacher picks up a pencil, then drops it to the floor.

TEACHER: Why did the pencil fall down?

KYLE: Because you dropped it.

(More muffled laughter.)

TEACHER:	I know, but why didn't it fall upward? Why does everything fall downward when it falls?
ANNE:	'Cause it's heavy.
TEACHER:	Mm, well, that's right, but heavier than what?
MICHELE:	Oh, I know! I know! Heavier than air.
TEACHER:	You're right! That's good. Heavier than air, which hardly weighs anything, and so objects fall through the air. In fact, almost every-thing is heavier than air. But can you think of something that's heav-ier than air and doesn't fall down?
DAVID:	Is it in this room?
TEACHER:	Well, not the thing I was thinking of, but let's see, there is at least one thing in this room that could be like that.
ANNE:	How about an airplane? They're heavy.
MICHELE:	Birds!
TEACHER:	That's right, too.
KYLE:	And balloons!
TEACHER:	Well, sort of. That's actually the thing I was thinking of that's in this room. But you must do something to a balloon to keep it from falling.
MICHELE:	Yes, blow it up.
TEACHER:	Yes, but not just with air. David, go get one of the balloons and blow it up, and we'll see if it stays in the air.

On the floor, three children and the teacher's aide have a map of the United States spread out in front of them. Each child has a small toy car with which to make a simulated trip on the map.

AIDE:	Why do we sometimes need maps?
JANET:	To see where we are going.
AIDE:	That's true. And how do we do that?
DONNICA:	Well, if we wanted to go to Pennsylvania, we'd get a map and see which roads would take us there, and then we'd go on those roads.
AIDE:	Great. That's really good. How come you know about Pennsylvania?
DONNICA:	Because that's where my grandma and grandpa live, and we drove there last summer.
AIDE:	Well, that's a very good reason for making a long trip like that. I bet your parents used maps to help them find the way. Tell you what—can you all think of a place in the United States where somebody lives that you would like to visit? (*All three children nod their heads.*) OK. Then let's put our cars here on the map, in Denver, where we are now. Let's see, can anyone find Denver?
JOHN:	Here it is. It's kinda right in the middle of the map.
AIDE:	Yes, it is. Let's all put our cars right on Denver. (*All place their cars.*) Now find the road you need, and then drive your car to the place you would like to visit.

(*After much studying of the map to find their locations, and some help from the teacher's aide, eventually the children get their cars to their destinations.*)

AIDE:	Well, it looks as if we all made it. Let's see now, who made the longest trip?
JANET:	Looks like John did.
DONNICA:	Wow! He went a long way!
JOHN:	This is where *my* grandma and grandpa live—here in New York City. To get to their house you gotta cross this big bridge. I mean it's really a giant thing. My dad says it's the biggest in the world, I think. He called it a stupendous bridge.
DONNICA:	A what?
JOHN:	Well—it's sort of, well, I mean—it's got these wires, like big pieces of rope, that hold it up.
AIDE:	Could you draw us a picture of one?
JOHN:	Yes, I think so.
AIDE:	Great. After we talk about our trips, if you'd like, we'll go over to the table and build some bridges out of boxes and see what we can learn about them.

A Behavioristic Third Grade Classroom

Most of the space in this classroom is taken up by the permanent desks and chairs arranged in rows. There are "centers," however, just as in the humanistic classroom, although they are fewer in number and the materials at each center have an appropriate storage place. Even though it is very organized, the room somehow seems crowded. This class has no teacher's aide.

At the moment all the students are seated at their desks after having seen a filmstrip about planets. The teacher has followed up with a demonstration using a globe and flashlight to illustrate the movement of sun and earth in relation to each other and the earth's rotation on its axis.

TEACHER:	Now that you have seen the filmstrip and demonstration, who can tell me why we have a night?

(Most of the hands go up.)

TEACHER:	Yes, Nathan, do you know?
NATHAN:	Because the sun isn't shining.
TEACHER:	No, the sun is always shining. It didn't stop shining in the filmstrip, and I never turned off the flashlight to make a nighttime. *(Some hands go back up.)* Maria, do you know?
MARIA:	It sets.
TEACHER:	Well, that's what we call it. But what really happens is the the earth does something. Remember in the filmstrip when the sun was setting, what was the earth doing to make the sun set?
HOWARD:	It was turning! *(He calls out without raising his hand, and the teacher does not recognize him.)*
TEACHER:	Stacey, thank you for raising your hand. What is the answer?

28

STACEY: The earth was turning. I mean, it turns away from the sun, or at least the part of the earth we are on, and so the sun isn't shining on us anymore.

(Howard mumbles aloud that he had just said that, but the teacher still ignores him.)

TEACHER: That's exactly right, Stacey. Now, can someone show us again how this happens by using the flashlight and the globe? *(Some hands go up.)* Thank you for raising your hand, Troy. You may come forward and show the whole class.

The lesson concludes with questions and answers, and the teacher makes an assignment in a science workbook which is coordinated to the filmstrip. The class then disperses into preassigned groups, which go to centers for preassigned work, except for one group which remains seated and begins to work on the science assignment.

One of the children at the math center has a very difficult time sitting in his chair and concentrating on the work. He gets out of his seat several times and watches others in the room for a moment, then sits down to try to attend to the math problems. When he is sitting and working, the teacher comes over to him as often as possible to tell him how much it is appreciated that he is trying to solve the problems, and then gives appropriate assistance. When he is out of his chair, he is ignored by the teacher.

The teacher then goes to the reading center and talks with one of the students.

TEACHER: Donald, I know you are a few days behind in your reading assignment.

DONALD: Yes, I know. There doesn't seem to be enough time to get it all done here. All the other kids read faster, anyhow.

TEACHER: Well, I've got an idea. Why don't you get as much done today as you can. Then you can take your book home tonight, and if you get caught up, tomorrow I'll have a treat for you. Maybe a candy bar. Is it a deal?

DONALD: You bet it is!

TEACHER: Great. That's an agreement between just you and me.

After twenty minutes, the teacher indicates it is time for all groups to change to a new center. Students who have completed the assignment at their center take gold stars and stick them next to their names on a chart. At the new centers, all groups begin work on other assignments.

A Humanistic High School Golf Class

Students are dressed in street clothes. As they come into the class, each selects a golf club. Some go to an area where they begin hitting some practice balls, others move off to the side and practice their swing. Some students experiment with their grip and stance, a few go to a practice sand trap near the hitting area, and a few stand around talking. The teacher, dressed in casual street clothes, is with the students testing their grip and stance, helping each one individually, making suggestions but never actually telling them how to hold the club or how to stand. Students change from area to area at will; the teacher also moves from one group to another. Although there is much verbal interaction between teacher and students, the teacher does not demonstrate. Twenty minutes after the official start of the class, the teacher calls all the students together.

TEACHER: Yesterday I suggested to you some of the things which most people agree are important parts of a good golf swing. Today I'm going to ask you to do a strange thing. I want you to forget about all those details and let your mind and body be as relaxed as you possibly can. Put aside any attention you might give to complicated muscle movements, and free your body for a fluid swing. I want your mind to *allow* your body to feel relaxed. To do that you must free your mind from any concern about details. Forget about *thinking* how to move. If your mind *thinks* it can control your muscles, it will tighten some of the tendons and chords which will interfere with a natural swing. It will inhibit your muscles from stretching, and they will hold back on the flowing motion which is so important for a good golf swing. Let your mind be free. Then your swing will *happen.* Instead of trying to *make* it happen, just *let* it happen. Trust your body to know how to do it.

(Although the students seem a bit puzzled, nevertheless they are willing to listen.)

TEACHER: Now, find a space where you will not be hindering anyone else. *(All students spread out.)* OK. Now put your hands on the club in a way that is comfortable for you.

And now, this may sound weird, but I'd like you to tighten the muscles of your forearms and hands as hard as you can. Really squeeze the club.

Now relax them and feel the difference. Feel how good it is to have your hands and arms relaxed. Notice the sensation of having no tension in your muscles. Yet they feel sensitive, ready to respond.

Now, as you begin to swing the club, feel the rhythm of the motion— loose and flowing. Let your body go. Your mind is not in the way, not trying to figure out the best way. It is giving freedom to your body. Let your swing *happen.* Let your muscles be like a stream flowing out of the mountain, with no obstacles to stop its course.

(With that, several students laugh a bit, and Adam feels compelled to make a comment. As he speaks, a few students nod their heads in acknowledgment.)

ADAM: Ah—maybe this is unusual, but I really have a hard time following this. I mean, I've never played golf in my life, and I don't have any idea what a good swing is, much less letting myself do it. I really don't know what it is I'm supposed to let happen.

TEACHER: I can sure appreciate that, and I know exactly what you are saying. I felt the same way when I first tried this. But you must allow your body the privilege of learning. To do that you must let your mind be free of whatever it is you *think* you ought to know. Even those experienced players who might know which muscles control the swing must still let go of the mind so that they are not *telling* their muscles what to do. You have an advantage over them in that no one ever showed you exactly how to swing. No one has cluttered your mind with details. It's just like learning how to walk. No one ever *told* you

30

how to do it, and even if someone had tried, you wouldn't have known what the words meant anyhow. Yet you learned, because you didn't *think* about it. You couldn't. When you learned, it just occurred. It's the same with golf. You must let the natural impulses of your body take over. Keep away from any conscious attention to the *how*, and just do it. Every time you swing the club, your body will remember the kind of swing you took. If it feels tight and mechanical, then you will know you need to let go of your mind even more, so that you allow yourself to have a free and easy swing.

LINDA: I think I know what you're saying. I can do it without the ball. But as soon as I step up to a ball—I don't know, something happens. I swing differently when there's a ball to swing at.

TEACHER: Probably you are thinking in your mind that somehow you must *force* the ball into the air—that you must use a lot of *effort*. That's not true because the ball has very little weight; and when you are swinging the club, because of some definite laws of physics, the clubhead has a tremendous amount of power in it, and it will easily get the ball on its way. Take your attention away from the ball and focus it back on your swing. Let yourself have the feeling you already know, just like in the practice swing. Then, all that is happening is that you are letting a ball get in the way of your swing.

KATHY: I think this is gonna take awhile. I feel really tight when I swing.

TEACHER: We all feel that way sometimes. Maybe that's not really a discredit because it means we have our minds active as we swing. But we must give our muscles the faith they deserve for being able to get along without our brains.

(Students go back to swinging the clubs, trying to sense what the teacher has been saying. For the next few moments, the teacher offers no verbal reinforcement. Then, as the students continue swinging, the teacher periodically reminds them of the feeling of the motion.)

TEACHER: Keep your swing simple and natural. Take the club back only as far as your body allows, then let the flow of the swing build its own speed.

You are not a machine, but a human being with a system that can *feel* the smoothness of your swing.

Fall into a rhythm. Try not to be overly purposeful with your swing, but be sensitive to the free and flowing motion. Keep that good feeling inside your muscles.

Release all tension. Golf is a "touch" sport, and if you hold your muscles back, you will not be able to feel the sensation of it.

Swing outside your consciousness. *Experience* your swing. Let your senses inside your body be the receivers they were meant to be. Tune in to your own self.

A Behavioristic High School Golf Class

As the students arrive they stand around talking, waiting for the start of class. They are casually dressed, as is the teacher, who is talking with them. At the moment the class is to start officially, the teacher tells everyone to take a golf club and calls them all together.

TEACHER: Yesterday some of you tried swinging a golf club for the first time in your lives. I didn't say too much to any of you then because I wanted to see how everyone would swing. But today, before you develop any bad habits relating to the swing, you need to become accustomed to some of the basic techniques for a good golf swing. The most basic of all is to learn the proper grip. It may seem like only an incidental thing, but it is your only direct contact with the club, and it is your indirect contact with the ball. So it is essential that you learn a grip which is sound and dependable.

The proper grip is not an accidental thing. It has been developed through experimentation and analysis, and it is based on principles which make a great deal of mechanical sense. Actually, there is more than one accepted way of holding the club, but almost all professional golfers, who obviously use the best techniques known since it is their livelihood, use something called the overlapping grip. It is the one that I am going to teach you today.

Now, place the clubhead on the ground. Make sure the face of the club is at ninety degrees to you.

Put your hands on the club with me, and you will have the proper grip. First extend your left hand with the palm facing away from the direction you would hit the ball, then place it on the grip of the club just below the top end, as I have done.

Close your fingers so that the club lies across the second joint of your index finger, at an angle. This will give you a combination finger and palm grip in your left hand.

Now close your hand over the club. Your thumb should be slightly to the right of the top of the shaft, and the index finger should be separated from your other fingers slightly.

Next, put your right hand on the club as I am doing, with the palm facing toward the direction you want to hit.

Notice that I am holding the club mostly in the fingers of my right hand.

Now move your right hand closer to your left by taking the little finger and *overlapping* it over the index finger of your left hand.

(At this point many students have a difficult time with the finger placement, so the teacher circulates among the group to place the students' hands together. In some cases the teacher must literally force student's hands into the overlapping grip.)

TEACHER: All that needs to be done, now, to complete this grip is to fold your right hand over the thumb of your left. Extend the index finger of your right hand down the shaft of the club in a "trigger finger" fashion and keep your right thumb off the top of the handle, placing it slightly to the left.

(The students still seem confused by all this information, and the teacher circulates among them again, assisting each one. Again, some students need the teacher to physically place their hands on the club. Many indicate how uncomfortable it feels, and after the teacher has attended to all students, some respond.)

JERRY: Man, this really feels strange. I feel like I'm all tied up. It seems like it would be more natural to hold this thing just like a baseball bat.

TEACHER: I'm sure it does. That's what makes the proper grip one of the more difficult things to learn about golf, because it feels unnatural. If I left you all to yourselves, I'm sure most of you would not pick up the golf club in the fashion I've shown you, and yet this grip allows your hands and wrists to have more leverage and power than the grips most of you would use.

CONNIE: Really? That's amazing. I've just been swinging the club, and with this grip I feel like I've got to force my way through it. Before, when I held it any way that felt right, it seemed that the swing was, you know, more natural. Now it's a strain.

TEACHER: It's understandable that when you first learn the proper grip your swing will feel strange. But to develop an effective and repeatable swing you must start with sound basics. A good swing is a product of other factors, the most fundamental of which is how you hold the club. If no one had ever thought about the best way to grip the club, the top golfers and everyone else would probably all have different styles, and the swings would probably also be different. But a lot of people have studied this game and have come to conclusions about the most effective techniques. That's why almost all the top golfers in the world use this grip—because it's the most effective. And the top golfers want to know the most effective ways because they make their living at the game.

SUE: That may be fine for them, but I'm not going to be a professional golfer. I just want to play for enjoyment, and I think I ought to do what feels best for me if that's all I want out of golf.

TEACHER: Trust me, in a few weeks this grip will feel right. It will give you the sensation that you are holding a golf club instead of a baseball bat or an ax. You'll settle your hands into this grip quite naturally, and what will feel unnatural then is the grips that many of you would like to use now. What's more, if your main objective is to enjoy the game, I've never known anyone who didn't enjoy any sport more when playing it well. So you see, instead of just letting you use any old grip that may seem right for you, I'm really helping you to enjoy the game by showing you the best techniques for playing it well.

An Abstract of the Basic Differences

To recapitulate, certain fundamental disagreements divide the humanists and the behaviorists. Some of the more important ones follow. The basic contentions of humanism include:

- The centering of attention on the experience of people and thus a focus on experience as the primary phenomenon of learning
- Emphasis on such distinctively human qualities as choice, creativity, valuation, and self-realization
- Commitment to making the actual *process* of learning meaningful
- An interest in developing the positive potential in every person
- Ultimate concern with and value of the dignity and worth of every individual *as* an individual.

Humanistic schools are those where the environment encourages successful personal encounter; where ideas, facts, and feelings are openly expressed; where conflict is not hidden; where emotions share equal importance with intellect; and where learning activities are a combination of student interests and the goals of the school.

The basic contentions of behaviorism include:

- The intentional altering of human behavior in the direction of desired ends
- Emphasis on human responses that are directly observable and measurable
- Commitment to making education efficient in evolving students toward desirable end *products*
- An interest in developing usable skills in every person
- Ultimate concern with specific objectives and specific steps to achieve those objectives.

Behavioristic schools are those where the environment is scientifically arranged for efficient learning; where the students know exactly what their goals are; where individual achievement is openly rewarded; where the teacher is an acknowledged source of information and authority; and where the learning activities are sequentially structured for observable progress.

Separate, Then Together

The next two parts of this book present a more thorough analysis of humanistic and behavioristic educational principles, with particular emphasis on their application to physical education. The final section brings the two systems together in dual use for teachers of physical education.

CHAPTER 4

The Referent of Freedom

Much has been written on the subject of freedom throughout human history. Among the many writers and thinkers wrestling with this problem, Will Durant in *The Story of Civilization* (1968) concluded that humankind can never be truly free. Because of hereditary physical and psychological inequalities, external controls in the form of laws or government are necessary to check the growth of inequities. Consequently freedom is sacrificed in the process of maintaining equality. Desmond Morris in *The Human Zoo* (1969) explained human behavior in biological terms, contending that any struggle for freedom results from biological processes inherent in and automatic to the human organism, rather than from any "will" to be free. Thus we tend unconsciously to avoid or escape from aversive features of the environment (crime, crowding, pollution—even technology). Kahlil Gibran in *The Prophet* (1965) considered freedom a state of spirit, mind, and feeling—a liberation of the soul, or psychic freedom, rather than an escape or avoidance of something.

An important first recognition for humanistic teaching, then, is that freedom comes in a variety of forms—among them Durant's freedom from bureaucratic control, Morris's freedom from physical technology, and Gibran's freedom from psychological constraints. Thus one may be free from events, from things, and from psychic confinement.

Over the centuries, we have learned how to generate many of our own freedoms. We have constructed a technological civilization which allows us to be relatively free from uncomfortable events and environmental conditions. We can, for example, turn up the thermostat when the weather is cold, or we can swallow some pills to neutralize physical pain. We can move to the country to avoid the crunch of a city, or we can avoid heavy labor by finding a sedentary job. We can ride an escalator instead of climbing stairs, or we can push a button at night to have our coffee ready in the morning. We can choose not to wear seat belts; we can become an alcoholic; or we can tear up the national forests with a trail bike. We can, literally, be "free" about almost anything we want to do, at least in the sense that we can choose whether or not to do it.

Freedom in this sense is a kind of possession, in that it can be attained through effort (or noneffort, as the case may be). We seem to have a great propensity toward this kind of freedom, for we are constantly tending to escape from or avoid or even destroy any form of control which interferes with our attainment of such possessable freedom. Perhaps this is because essentially we know how to gain such freedom. There are also well-known ways to avoid certain unfree conditions of family life, or occupation, or friends, or religion, even government. But the literature is somewhat unclear about how to avoid the psychological condition of unfree *feelings*. We have never found an exact way to provide all people with the freedom of which Gibran speaks: freedom of the mind.

This is a more discrete kind of freedom, one which concerns humanism directly. It is a sort of "inner liberty"—a freedom of the inner person. It exists aside from any outward choices or alternatives which we may have from environmental situations. It does not refer to the daily decisions we make about physical and situational constraints in our lives (such as whether to take an aspirin for a headache or attend a disliked class). Instead, it implies a freedom of a far greater dimension. It is *subjective* rather than objective, *psychological* rather than physiological, *attitudinal* rather than behavioral.

This phenomenon could be masked by what might be called "attributed" freedom, where we are *told* that we are free and *given* such "freedom" as the right to lead a private life, the opportunity to choose a profession or to decide where to live—none of which guarantees a freedom of the psyche. In this respect, some educational theories have assumed that if students were provided with an "open" environment and the opportunity to make their own choices, they would automatically become liberated, happy, and creative persons. While such an environment may be a necessary beginning for total freedom, it does not assure that students will have the inner resources to know what to do with it. The environment alone cannot establish the self-reliance, the excitement with learning, the creative spirit, and all the other psychic operations which are the outcomes of a truly free mind.

It is true, however, that the environment *can* be a major factor in freedom. People *are* essentially products of their environmental stimuli. On that one particular point all educational philosophies are agreed—humanism even agrees with behaviorism. Accordingly, then, one of the foundational tasks of education is to define those conditions which are most *likely* to generate the attitudes which are the qualities of free states of mind.

Why are such definitions so important? First of all, the humanistic approach to education begins with freedom as the absolute prerequisite for all its objectives:

THE IMPORTANT LEARNING OUTCOMES OF HUMANISTIC EDUCATION (SELF-ACTUALIZATION AND THE LIKE) ARE POSSIBLE ONLY IN AN ENVIRONMENT WHICH PROMOTES FREEDOM OF MIND.

This inner, subjective, psychological, and attitudinal freedom predisposes to all other kinds of freedom.

How can the teacher create such a climate? It begins with a willingness—a readiness to *allow* freedom, which is more than the mere giving of permission to students to be more self-directive. It means a sacrifice of some presumed "control" over students, which must be made if one believes in the basic concept of humanism and wishes to use it in teaching.

Before we discuss the technique for establishing a free climate in education, it is first necessary to analyze more completely the nature of this inner freedom.

Freedom on the Inside

As we have seen, it is one thing to be free from famine, pestilence, pain, danger, and other physically uncomforatble situations. It is another thing to be free from governmental, cultural, and societal constraints. It is still another thing to be free inside oneself.

Inner freedom is difficult to describe. It is rather complex, but it cannot be ignored. Principally it comes in two forms, and in its application to physical education it involves a third consideration.

1. *Psychological Freedom.* The freedom to think, to feel, and to perceive is a condition which fosters the emergence of a more capable self. It is an *attitude* about being free, existing as a distinct state of mind which normally comes from the nature of the environment. Carl Rogers (1969) has said that such a state of "feeling free" can be a reality only when the complete educational environment allows students to express their feelings, impulses, and percepts without fear of punishment for doing so. Psychological freedom, then, is the *result* of an environment intentionally arranged to permit full expression of values. It allows for the openness, spontaneity, and creativity which are released with a freeing of the inner spirit.

Such is the condition of the "open" schools. When the teacher, or an entire school, allows for the complete freedom of symbolic expression, students are presumed to become more at liberty to be their own selves, to pursue their own interests, and to determine their own values. Thus the fundamental air of open education is to assist students in developing an independence of thought—not a general antagonism to all ideas outside their own frame of reference, but a positive receptivity to all ideas and an ability to discriminate among them freely and symbolically. And this capacity, as we shall see later, can be generated through physical education.

The basic criterion of psychological freedom, then, is that students be allowed the freedom to *think* anything and to *express* their thoughts without the potential of being told they are wrong. It must be recognized, however, that sometimes this free expression must be made *symbolically.* There are certain behaviors which, if overtly executed, would result in harm to others. Psychological freedom therefore permits *thinking* about all emotions and sensations, but it forbids any action which could result in a reduction of the psychological freedom of other persons. Thus, while a student may think about hitting someone else, or disrupting a class, or breaking the windows in the school, such acts are forbidden on the ground that they interfere with the freedom of others. While psychological freedom is a total allowance for the liberal wanderings of the mind, then, it also implies the *responsibility* to outwardly respect the freedom of others.

Probably the most important element of such psychological freedom is that the environment must be nonjudgmental. The teacher cannot constantly tell students they are right or wrong. There must be a *feeling* that each person is the authority for individual decisions. To accomplish this the teacher must lay aside any judgments about opinions that students may express. Rather, students must sincerely *feel* and *know* they are free to think and respond in their own ways and with their own intuitions. This is a psychological *sensation* of being mentally liberated, unlimited, ungoverned, and uncompelled.

2. *Intellectual Freedom.* Closely related to psychological freedom is the concept of intellectual freedom. Whereas the former is essentially an attitude and a feeling about freedom from externally imposed constraints, intellectual freedom is the condition whereby students are *encouraged* to think in a self-reliant and original fashion.

First there must be a *sense* of being free—an internal feeling of independence which teachers can establish by taking the threats out of the environment. Intellectual freedom then specifically relates to the *fostering* of expressions of original thought and the generation of creativity. Psychological freedom may be thought of as an *allowance*, intellectual freedom as an *expectation*.

Perhaps an illustration will add some clarity. Suppose for a moment that your hobby is photography. You do it on your own, when you feel like it, with themes of your own choosing, and with no feeling of compulsion or commitment. One can then say that you have complete psychological and intellectual freedom in this interest, since there are no constraints and you are responsible to no one but yourself. Your own spontaneity is the sole guide for the directions you take in your hobby. Then, assume that your interest develops to the point that you believe you would enjoy using it as a vocation and you do indeed find employment as a professional photographer. What was formerly an interest of complete independence now becomes a responsibility. There is now a demand, however subtle, to satisfy certain job requirements. You are now under obligation to provide results which are probably dictated by your employer. No longer can you give in completely to your own impulses. Thus some of the psychological freedom which was yours when photography was a hobby is now lost, replaced by the particular mechanisms of a job responsibility. This may, in turn, be reflected in a reduction of intellectual freedom, for it is likely that you must now attend to the themes assigned by your employer instead of acting on your own intuition. Essentially, then, intellectual freedom will have suffered some confinement by the very structure of the job. Psychological freedom will also have been severely curtailed by the fact that the job demands time commitments in prescribed amounts and products of prescribed quality.

As it is, total psychological and intellectual freedom are probably rarely achieved in a vocational setting. Schools, however, are in a far better position to grant both. The open education movement has been relatively successful in providing the atmosphere for students to think, reason, and express their impulses without fear of reprisal. Humanistic philosophy has always promoted educational conditions free from any suppression of the psyche, and also encouraged being self-generative in thought, with no compulsion for channeling one's thinking into prescribed directions.

3. *Movement Freedom*. The third freedom concerns physical education more directly. In broad perspective, movement freedom is the allowance and the encouragement to be expressive through the use of the body medium. This freedom has had a considerable influence on the direction taken by physical education in recent times.

Generally viewed, most physical movement is habitual (walking, running). Or it can have a definite and prescribed function, as in the performance of specific sports skills. Or it can be a subjective and subconscious representation of our states of mind. However bodily actions are seen, it is now an accepted standard that the mind and the body operate as a unit. There is no longer a question as to whether there is a mind and body separate—mental and physical phenomena are interrelated, one dependent on and influencing the other. This mind/body linkage is very important for humanistic physical education.

The ramification of this harmony between mind and body (to be discussed more specifically later) begins with the fact that there is ample evidence (Field 1970; Lengyel 1971; Lytton 1972; Gowan 1972; Hearn, Burdin, and Katz 1972; Schroder, Karlins, and Phares 1973; Spodek and Walberg 1975; Arieti 1976; Aspy and Roebuck 1977) that when the educational atmosphere is one of freedom, the resulting intellectual liberty will enable students to be more original and creative. When teachers minimize rules and encourage discovery and self-appropriated learning, then education is fostering the kinds of freedom that result in more meaningful knowledge—generally referred to as conceptual learning. Moreover, an atmosphere of psychological and intellectual freedom appears to assist students in becoming organized, consistent, and self-controlled human beings.

There is no question, then, that

WHEN EDUCATION PROVIDES AN ATMOSPHERE OF FREEDOM, STUDENTS TEND TO BECOME MORE SELF-RELIANT AND CREATIVE.

Therefore, it is easy to carry the logic into the physical domain, for—

1. Since psychological and intellectual freedom appear to facilitate self-discovered and creative learnings in mental matters, and
2. Since the mind and the body are so closely related to each other, then
3. These same self-appropriated and creative impulses can be manifested *motorically*.

Not only is it possible that creativity can be *expressed* through a motor medium, but it may also be possible that the motoric expression of creativity can actually *increase* the general ability to be creative in *any* fashion. In other words, self-expression in one medium may assist self-expression in another medium. Thus if a student is encouraged to be creative in physical education, the inner and self-discovered benefits learned in this manner will transfer to a more creative aptitude in art, music, language, and other endeavors. (Some evidence does exist. See Arieti 1976.)

39

In this context, self-actualization becomes a major objective of physical education, and the instructional technique becomes related to providing the conditions which will foster individuality and self-discovery. This means that physical education must exist in a setting of psychological and intellectual freedom, with the added allowance for the motoric interpretation of inner thoughts and feelings. Students must be given the freedom to be expressive within themselves through the use of their own bodies. Furthermore, it will also be seen that this attitude can be used for the teaching of specific sports skills. Freedom does not simply provide a liberty for the expression of inner feelings without the recognition of any potential for motor skill learning. Nor does it work only in the lower grades. Its dimensions and its spirit can be a distinct assist to *all* persons, regardless of age, in the learning of skilled motor achievement.

Unfortunately, psychological, intellectual, and movement freedoms are not so commonly found in physical education programs. All too often, constraints such as the following are imposed on students, resulting in a loss of much spontaneity in self-discovered learnings.

1. A prescribed curriculum gives at least the implication that all students should learn the same motor activities.
2. Standardized tests compare all students to some norm, not to themselves.
3. Such tests also reflect other-imposed values rather than student interests, with grades assigned by such values instead of attained by each student relative to the self.
4. The teaching of specific movement patterns implies that all students are anatomically and neurologically identical and will therefore learn motor skills in exactly the same way.

A humanistic approach to physical education cannot tolerate such mistakes. To do so would be an injustice to the rights of students and a violation of their individuality and would impose a program of "doing" rather than "being," thereby distorting the very essence of the profession.

All People Are Cast in Different Molds

No matter how trite it may sound, all people *are* individuals—an obviously supportive fact for humanism, which not only recognizes but promotes individuality.

To begin with, all persons are anatomically different. Within that difference, some people have been born with a body type which predisposes them for potential success in particular motor skills, while others have been born with a body type which places a limitation on them for the attainment of such success (Hebbelinck and Ross 1974). Unfortunately, most of us are born with a sort of "have-not" body type, for seventy percent of the range of variable types of bodies in the world are never seen in Olympic performers (Leonard 1975). This fact alone may be enough to declare the unfairness of any prescribed curriculum or standardized testing, because in any standardized situation most persons are relegated to comparative failure.

Furthermore, the manner in which we receive, interpret, and respond to our environment is different in each of us. We do not all agree exactly on what we see, hear, and feel from our surroundings. Sensory phenomena vary with individuals; thus all will perceive the same controlled light stimulus with different perceptions about its intensity or feel different sensations from an auditory stimulus. Our tolerance of pain differs; the way we respond to stress varies considerably. Most importantly, our motor organization shows us to be very individualistic in every respect (see especially Leukel 1978).

The foregoing differences argue for an educational environment which provides the necessary freedoms for students to be individuals. An intriguing bonus may be the possibility that by removing the constraints placed on students by older methods of teaching, the learning situations in physical education will take on a much needed outcome of freedom—that is, a great quality of *relief*. Rather than feeling they are being judged by some remote and unreasonable standard or average, students will then feel they are being seen and valued for themselves, with the teacher making decisions relative to the innate potentials of each individual.

Giving classes back to the students through the provision of freedom will promote a renewed sense of significant, self-fulfilling, experiential learning. Student attention (and possibly that of teachers as well) will do an inversion, going from externally constructed and imposed values to *personal involvement* in the learning process. The whole person—mind and body in combination—will take on a genuine feeling of being *in* the learning environment, with the values *internal* to the students. The very essence of learning will in fact be in the actual learning itself, as the *process* becomes more important than what is achieved.

Freedom Is Not Free Play

The principle of providing freedom for students sometimes appears so effortless that it can lull us into a potential blind faith that all that is needed is to be a sort of "nice person," or to show compassion, or to be fair or some other magical quality. Or we can deceive ourselves into thinking that if we throw out the basketballs (where have we heard *that* before?) and retreat to the office to be out of the students' way, we have satisfied the requirements of freedom. Such a reaction, however, is collective amnesia about something called responsibility. An honest freedom-oriented physical education has a commitment to *purpose*—involving planning, disposition, progression, and that notable trait of all successful teachers, organization.

Movement freedom in particular does not imply the kind of liberty which is mere free play. Instead, it is the encouragement for students to experience the full potential and variability of movement responses of which they are capable. It is a motoric self-actualization, and it occurs only when there is a *facilitation* of movement experimentation.

41

It must be continually remembered that the ultimate objective of any physical education program, no matter how open and freedom-based it may be, is to enhance the physical abilities of students. Humanistic analogy does not disagree. It simply states that the process of skill attainment is rooted in *discovery*, not in a teacher *telling* students how to perform. Humanistic physical education is based on the conviction that motor skill learning grows *from* movement. It is the experience *in* and experimentation *of* movement which provide the grounds for the development and refinement of motor skills. The greatest accomplishment in such an approach to physical education is that students learn to feel, to kinesthetically sense, their own movement activities. This is a very specific declaration of the concept of "knowing oneself," for to know oneself kinesthetically is to know oneself internally, and to know oneself internally is a primary objective of all humanistic education.

Freedom in Summary

Being free can mean merely having uncommitted time; it can exist as a "nothingness." In contrast, psychological, intellectual, and movement freedoms exist as a "somethingness" which is both a provision *for* and an enlistment *of* learning. Freedom is thus expressed as a capacity, for in a freedom-based education students are less likely to think in terms of "What *must* I do?" and more likely to think in terms of *allowance* and *encouragement*. This is a psychological *feeling* and an intellectual and motoric *stimulation* for self-discovered learnings.

It may sometimes be a difficult environment to create, but certainly not an impossible one. The important question now becomes—HOW?

CHAPTER 5

The Facilitation of Humanistic Teaching

Freedom works slowly. It requires patience, the courage to see it through, and preparation. It also requires trust, from both teachers and students, and an acceptance of the adjustments often necessary in the early stages. It is not so much the mere presence of freedom that is important, however, as its nature and the manner in which it is granted. Freedom cannot be given as a sudden allowance, particularly in settings which are presently unfree. It is not an absolute to be handed out at will with instant results. In fact, when given as an unexpected allowance, it may actually result in effects which are the opposite of those desired (Hart 1970) and may even produce student rebellion (Rice and Cramer 1977).

Fundamentally, students should be given only as much freedom as they can handle, within their sense of responsibility and capacity to function. Random freedom, without purpose, simply does not work. When provided in gradually increasing quantities, however, freedom will encourage students to accept the responsibility and share in its directions. Ideally, students will become essentially self-governing.

Realistically granted, freedom *does* work, and it appears to result in the self-reliant student impulses valued by humanistic educators.

Letting Go

There may be one major initial difficulty. Creating an environment of psychological, intellectual, and movement freedom, with little or no constraint and few rules, may be inconsistent with many teachers' ideas of the educational process. Permitting an attitude of freedom to exist requires that teachers sacrifice some of their "power" status and meet students on more equal grounds. Consequently:

TEACHERS WITH PERSONALITIES THAT INCLUDE STRONG NEEDS FOR CONTROL MAY NOT BE ABLE TO ACCEPT SOMETHING WHICH TO THEM IMPLIES DISORGANIZATION AND A GREAT POTENTIAL FOR DISRUPTION.

Such teachers are more likely to equate freedom with chaos, a free atmosphere with loss of conrol, and therefore a loss of status with students.

This may be especially true in physical education. By the very nature of its content and setting, physical education tends to foster more volatility in students—more noise, interaction, movement, and so forth. Such spontaneous happenings can be interpreted as a loss of the regulation that some teachers believe to be more necessary in physical education than in other disciplines.

Additionally, teachers may reinforce each other's controlling behaviors (usually subconsciously) through informal discussions on the various ways of conducting classes. The lunch room, the teachers' lounge, and other meeting places can become planning stations for the exchange of ideas and idiosyncratic "secrets" about class control. Consequently teachers may directly reaffirm to each other that control is an essential of the occupation.

Further, even the students can be a factor in prompting the use of control procedures by teachers. When given freedom which did not exist previously, students may supply the permitting teacher with such subtle comments as "Better not let the principal see you do this," or "No one else lets us get away with this," or "You won't last long around here, you're too nice." The events then set in motion may move the teacher back to more traditionalistic control. Thus there may be a compromise in favor of maintaining student serenity, or faculty status quo, or even one's job. And humanism becomes the loser.

It's All Part of the Scene

A professional teaching career is a demanding endeavor. Students, curriculum, administration, other teachers, and perhaps even parents may sometimes appear overwhelming. It is easy to understand that teachers may feel the need to establish some sort of "position" as a defense to these factors. The most expedient method is to resort to measures of authoritarianism. Research presented by Dunkin and Biddle (1974) indicates that the more insecure the teacher feels about any threat to leadership, the more likely that teacher will use tactics of control. Furthermore, there appears to be an inherent and conscious feeling on the part of most teachers that "something ought to be happening" within their classes; consequently there is a subtle pressure for more dominant and directive regulation than a freedom-based atmosphere seems to provide. Also of interest in this regard is the research of Walberg (1967), who found that a common circumstance in beginning a professional teaching career is a dramatic reduction in self-esteem. This reaction appears to be an outcome of the teacher's realization that preconceived ideals about the effects of education on students' lives may have been overestimated. Resultingly, in an effort to "make things happen" more rapidly, the teacher reacts with domination. Dreeben (1973) has presented research which indicates that this loss of self-esteem may be due to the fact that education is too much involved in matters which make it a "workplace" as well as a learning center. As a result, the nonteaching functions (filing reports, keeping records, grading tests) tend to animate teachers into a more mechanistic attitude toward the totality of the profession.

Significantly, there is apparently an even greater tendency for physical education teachers to employ command methods in their classes than is evidenced in other subject areas. Perhaps this is an outgrowth of the fact that physical education is an active affair, with more potential for disorder and accidents. It may also be due in part to the psychological characteristics of those persons who enter the profession. Kenyon (1965) and Hendry (1973) have shown that physical education teachers possess more traditional ideas about education than other teachers. In fact, physical educators tend to be more psychologically similar to persons in business fields than to other educators. On this basis it may be concluded that they probably feel uncomfortable in settings that allow the freedoms which are the foundation of humanistic teaching. Dunkin and Biddle (1974) show evidence that there may be some relation to the fact that teacher preparing institutions are themselves traditionalistic. We may therefore conclude that

IT MAY BE MORE DIFFICULT TO ESTABLISH HUMANISTIC TEACHING IN PHYSICAL EDUCATION THAN IN OTHER DISCIPLINES.

Teachers who *do* approach physical education with a freedom-giving attitude seem to be manifesting personality traits that were part of their makeup before they chose the profession (Hendry 1970). These teachers sometimes face serious resistance from other faculty members, or the general atmosphere of the shool, or even students (Dunkin and Biddle 1974).

A Gradual Ascent into Freedom

If we were to draw any conclusion based on the number of books recently written and the number of articles appearing in professional journals, unquestionably that conclusion would have to be that there is a widespread and sincere interest in utilizing the philosophy of humanism in physical education. Indeed, it appears that

IN RECENT YEARS PROFESSIONAL PHYSICAL EDUCATION HAS MADE A CONCERTED EFFORT TO INCLUDE HUMANISTIC PRINCIPLES IN ITS TEACHING METHODOLOGY.

The literature proffers innumerable suggestions as to exactly how to go about introducing humanistic arrangements into a setting not presently humanistic. Since there is little research in this area, however, it is necessary to listen to the empirical opinions of those who have been on the real scene (those who have taught in the schools) along with those who may never have taught in the schools but who write books and articles. Although the quantity of suggestions is enormous and the range of advice wide, there seems to be a central point of agreement in all the literature:

THE MOST COMMON SUGGESTION IN THE LITERATURE ON HOW TO DEVELOP AN ATMOSPHERE OF FREEDOM IN AN OTHERWISE UNFREE EDUCATIONAL SETTING CAN BE SUMMED UP IN ONE WORD—GRADUALLY.

It is generally agreed that any sudden declaration of independence for previously formal classes will usually be met with instant failure. The students themselves, the greatest benefactors of humanism, may not be able to accept the sudden responsibility for self-direction given by a well-intentioned teacher. More realistically, the bestowal of freedom should occur in gradually increasing allowances, directly proportional to the ability of students to handle the new freedoms. It may logically be concluded that the more formal and traditionalistic the present educational atmosphere, the more gradual the giving of freedom should be.

Getting Freedom Under Way

Although the question of *how* to implement humanistic teaching methods has never been a subject of pure research, there is much *opinion* available. Havelock (1969), who assembled four thousand of these opinions, concluded that the worst thing to do was to make sudden *drastic* changes in the prevailing class orientation. In a sense, then, the less innovative an innovation, the more likely it is to be successful. This does not mean that one should use only "non-innovative" techniques, but that any innovation must proceed gradually. On that basis, the following recommendations can be made:

1. *Bits and Pieces.* It is necessary to start by experimenting with small, self-contained dispensings of freedom. Less formal roll call, a reduction in the number of class rules, discarding the whistle, more tolerance of minor disturbances, allowing students to aid in developing objectives, and other concessions—all may assist in the transfer to a more open feeling. In some cases, when specific rules are to be changed, it may help for the teacher to make perfectly clear to students which rules will change and the reasons for change. Cole (1972) has shown that policy changes generally work best when students have been given a prechange readiness. With such preparation both teacher and students appear to be more willing to give the new policies a fair trial; furthermore, classes also seem prepared for future alterations in management.

It is also necessary to "hold" the class at each new stage of progressive freedom until it becomes clear that the class is able, at that stage, to assume a sense of order, equity, and responsibility. This is another advantage for giving gradual allowances—one is not committed to a total alteration, and it is therefore easier to back off a bit if necessary.

2. *Purposeful Allowances.* The teacher must make clear to students that there is a purpose within any new liberty. It cannot just be hollow free time; rather, it must be an allowance for working more independently on specific projects. Thus more responsibility is placed on students. As a giving of intellectual freedom, a new liberty is given as a stimulus.

Moreover, there is some evidence (Borton 1970) that when freedom is given without purpose, it results in the rather strange side effect of increasing student antagonism toward *each other*. On the other hand, when the new freedom includes an understanding of the inherent responsibilities, the problem of student aggression is drastically reduced.

3. *Implicit Feelings.* Freedom must carry with it an *attitude* about the process. It must be given without strain and received without conflict. When this is comprehended by both the giving teacher and the receiving students, there is a mutual psychological and intellectual understanding. Any insincerity will be found out; there can be no pretending about it. This means there are many *implications,* for the attitude itself must exist without the demand for verbal verifications. Thus, while it is advisable to *tell* students that particular rules or policies are to be changed, it is not necessary (and may be impossible) to explain the *feeling* underlying the changes. This must come instead as an impression which is developed through the *process* of opening up the class.

Briefly, then, the gradual evolution into an atmosphere of freedom appears to involve three basic considerations:

1. A FREE ATMOSPHERE BEGINS WITH PARTS OF THE WHOLE. INITIAL FREE-DOMS SHOULD BE GIVEN ONLY IN QUANTITIES THAT STUDENTS CAN RESPONSIBLY RECEIVE.

2. MEANING SHOULD BE PROVIDED WITHIN THE GIVING OF FREEDOM BY SHOWING STUDENTS THAT AN INCLUDED PURPOSE IS TO ALLOW FOR INDIVIDUAL VARIANCES IN LEARNING AND MORE SELF-RELIANCE.

3. IF FREEDOM CANNOT BE GIVEN SINCERELY AND WITH CONVICTION, IT SHOULD NOT BE GIVEN.

When it all works, the allowances are recognized by students and are attitudinally received, student responsibility is increased, potential repercussions are minimized and possibilities for positive results maximized.

Sources of Information

Students are excellent sources for recognizing which freedoms they may be most in need of. One need merely ask them. Their intital answers will generally come as some form of "relief" from whatever autocracies are currently in effect. Occasionally we all have difficulty getting outside ourselves, seeing things from other people's perspective. Thus, by asking students their opinions, certain constraining events which otherwise may not have been noticed will become clear. Further, when students have a voice in the new directions to be taken, they are more likely to give whole-hearted cooperation to the changes. Anything resembling "homework" in this process will mean that students will need to practice the common concerns of humanistic behavior *outside* the class, with at least a theoretical possibility that they may incorporate such concerns into their overall lives.

It must also be understood that freedom does not limit itself to positives. To be open to growth is to be open to setbacks as well. Allowing students the freedom to express themselves openly also includes an allowance for them to criticize. Honesty, when fostered, can bring some hurt along with it. Students must know, however, that if they are truly open and sometimes critical, they will not be punished—even though it may sometimes be difficult for the teacher to absorb all their opinions.

Physiological Internalization

A very intriguing result of a humanistic educational system is the potential it gives students to maximize their capacity for response variability. They can become flexible in their ability to adjust to changes in the environment and also able to generate their own internal responses. These outcomes are manifested through an *inward* rather than an outward view of existence. Students become more a part of themselves, more expressive, more creative, more in control of their own behavioral systems. And this presents a fascinating possibility in physical education. If we begin with the theory that the ultimate objective of a humanistic approach to physical education is to enable students to internalize their perceptions, then we must concur that the freedom for movement expression can specifically produce *kinesthetic* internalizations. Very realistically, the encouragement of motor experimentation brings student attention inward, to the sensations that arise from within their own muscles. They experience an increased perception of movement and an internalization which are potentially the most influential of all factors in motor skill learning. This important matter is discussed at greater length later in this book.

CHAPTER 6

The Process Within

Humanistic education cannot live by freedom alone. An extreme, too-open approach to learning does not work. Those schools which have tried it have been short-lived, lasting an average of only nine months (Kozol 1972), mostly because they provided *only* freedom, nothing else.

A relatively structure-free atmosphere is a first prerequisite of humanistic endeavors, but for ultimate success there must be some substance within. Artful teaching is achieved through planned learning experiences, not through the mere provision of freedom. Self-actualization rarely occurs without environmental stimulation (Aspy and Roebuck 1977). The teacher, then, becomes the most important ingredient for success, for the catalyst of learning originates from the educational experiences designed by the teacher.

Often, such experiences may take on a rather curious aspect. For example, the teacher may ask students to fantasize themselves inside a strange object, to think of themselves as a political leader, to imagine themselves an outer-space visitor to earth, to invent new ways of using a common piece of string, to take a tour of their own uninhibited daydreams or any other imagining which will give a different perspective to their lives. In physical education, students may engage in the silent improvisations of a free expressive dance; or exaggerate spontaneous body movements; or imagine themselves an animal, an object, a force, or any other variety of motor expression not usually manifested in conventional teaching.

The intent of humanistic education is to increase the number of channels of communication, external and internal, available to students for their development and exploration. It is an attempt to break down the barriers of narrow ways of viewing things, people, and oneself. In its consummate form, humanistic education becomes a *process* of seeing, of becoming, of being.

Two Kinds of Learning: Content and Process

Traditional education considers academic excellence its major goal. It has been mainly concerned with the "what," the "how much," and the "how fast" of learning. Its emphasis has been placed on raw *information*, which is usually measured by tests or some other academic standard showing the *quantity* factors of student accomplishments.

The requirements for *living*, however, are far more *psychological* than mechanical. Information, by itself, is necessary as a basis of operation, but life is a *process*—an ongoing flow of assimilating, organizing, and using basic information. These are the intangible events of life—the perceptions, the abstracts, the feelings. Humanistic education attends more to *how* people learn rather than to *what* they learn: the *process* of learning is more important than the learning itself. Thus, while traditional education centers on the *content*, humanistic education gives its attention to the events inherent in the *process*.

Content Education Is Easy

Parents do it. Books do it. Advertisements do it. Machines do it. Teachers do it. We all do it at some time or another.

Providing content is often a simple matter. It amounts to giving facts, codes, propaganda, or announcements to any receiving person for storage and retrieval at some appropriate time in the future. For example, when learning to count to ten, or to recite the alphabet, or to read, a child first performs by rote. There is not yet any concept of how numbers relate to each other, or how letters can be rearranged to form words, or how words in sentences can form different meanings. Probably such fixed, mechanical acquisitions are the only way early learnings can realistically occur, but often the emphasis may remain on this pattern of learning after the basic information has been acquired.

In physical education, a content approach occurs when the teacher demonstrates a particular motor skill and then requires students to attempt a replication of the demonstration, without allowance for variation. Achievement is measured relative to accomplishment of the storybook standard, or, worst of all, by comparison with other students in the class. Learning thus becomes a passive reception of information, external to the inner resources of students. Emphasis is *outside* the existence of the learners.

In truth, content education is a highly effective way of achieving results. As a matter of expediency it is easier; it requires less versatility in teaching, less ingenuity in planning, and less consideration for individual variance, than process education. According to Schroder, Karlins, and Phares (1973), content teaching has three characteristics:

1. A fixed teaching pattern
2. Emphasis on passive learning
3. Little (if any) student/teacher interaction.

Whereas content-centered education tends to emphasize external factors, process-centered education aims at the development of the inner person. Relying on externals, the former is conducive to authoritarian and autocratic teaching methods; the latter, in contrast, allows students to be the authors of their own learning.

Although content education does have some desirable outcomes, when the *complete* emphasis is placed on volume learning with prescribed times, students will not acquire the creative and adaptive abilities necessary for using information in the real world. Conclusively, then, the overall effect of content education can be seen in a series of generally negative consequences which follow.

1. *Student dependency on others rather than self-reliance is developed.* Information gathering overrules information processing. Students in physical education become conditioned to depending on the teacher for all information and feedback about performances instead of attending to their internal, kinesthetic resources which they could learn to use as individual feedback systems.

2. *Motivation is external rather than internal.* The teacher determines what student interests should be. Therefore a genuine intrinsic regard for the joy of learning is less likely to evolve. Such an attitude in physical education leads to the mistaken idea that students really want drills in basketball fundamentals for twelve consecutive years.

3. *Learning is irrelevant rather than relevant.* Any learning which is relevant can be effectively, resourcefully, and flexibly used in life. Standing on a prescribed spot for roll call is not such a learning; nor is having to respond constantly to a whistle; nor the suppression of individuality.

4. *Students become resolute rather than adaptable.* Content education tends to foster an avoidance of uncertainty. But much of life is fluid, changing from moment to moment, with inherent uncertainties. This is also the case with motor performance. Effective sports performance is a matter of constant adaptability to changing situations. Such abilities are less likely to develop when all students are expected to perform skills in the same prescribed fashion.

5. *Evaluation is standardized rather than individualized.* In physical education the evaluation of achievement often takes the form of how many, or how often, or how accurately. A test which measures how many baskets a student can make in one minute is unindividualistic; and requiring students to hit tennis balls into a marked area on the court does not tell much about overall playing ability.

6. *Insecurity rather than flexibility of both teacher and students is developed.* Since it is based on uniformities and dependables, content education tends to develop a strange form of security. When taken away from such a standardized setting, both teacher and students may feel insecure and uncertain. Physical education is particularly vulnerable, because the nature of the setting (greater frequency of noise and movement) often conditions teachers into imposing more rigid controls on students.

In summary, content-centered education reduces spontaneity, interest, curiosity, and creativity. It tends to increase narrow-mindedness, intolerance, conventionalism, and aggressiveness. Humanistic education cannot allow such injustices.

A Less Travelled Road—Process Education

In the time-honored practice of content learning, the student who is given a problematical situation pulls out a prepackaged rule or concept stored as memory and uses it on the problem. This is a utilization of rote.

In process learning, on the other hand, the student is encouraged to create concepts instead. Here is a test of such an ability:

> A man and his two sons must cross a stream in a small boat. The man weighs 200 pounds and each son weighs 100 pounds. The boat can carry only 200 pounds. How will they get across the stream?

To arrive at a solution, you must ponder the facts without trying to fit them into some preconceived judgment. You must have a "feel" for the problem and reason it out intuitively. (The answer: The two sons cross first, then one son goes back and gets off the boat. Dad rows over alone, gets off, and the other son returns to pick up his brother.) Too easy? Try this one:

> On the basis of the information given by the following three cubes, can you tell the arrangement of the dots on the bottom of cube 3?

1.   **2.**   **3.**

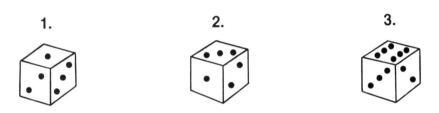

Here you cannot, obviously, pull out a prepared answer. You must be able to organize information from several vantage points, abstractly picking up the cubes and rotating them visually. You must be both perceptive and receptive, even though the information may appear conflicting. For example, suppose you are told that the three cubes shown are not standard dice. Are your first perceptions now unreliable? If so, it is necessary to change your way of discerning the situation. Note that on cubes 1 and 3 the two-dot and the three-dot sides are in different relationship to each other. Does that make it seem that you cannot be seeing different views of the same cube? But these are not real dice, so on further abstraction, it is still possible that one cube is being viewed three ways. (That is in fact the case. For the answer see p. 55.)

These examples point out, rather playfully, that a certain kind of intelligence is not necessarily related to concrete functions. It is a more open, receptive, flexible, abstract, and inventive kind of mental ability—an aptitude for logical and analytical thought, a capacity to get *outside* a situation to see it more clearly. There is nothing unusual about such an ability. Everyone has it to some extent. It is the same resource one uses when creating a written composition, or planning a home redecoration project, or painting a picture. It is the kind of intelligence needed to respond to the flowing motion and constant changes of a soccer or basketball game. And it has a name—*fluid* intelligence—and is to be distinguished from its opposite, *crystallized* intelligence.

An Intelligence for Motor Performance

Memorizing a poem is an example of crystallized intelligence; understanding the meaning of the poem demonstrates fluid intelligence. Crystallized intelligence is "book learning." Fluid intelligence is conceptualization. Crystallized intelligence is rote. Fluid intelligence is common sense. People who have a high degree of crystallized intelligence can deal with concretes and absolutes: two and two is four, the moon is 240,000 miles away, red and blue mixed together make purple. Those who have a high degree of fluid intelligence can think in abstracts: $2 \times 10^6/5 \times 10^2 = 4 \times 10^3$, outer space is infinite, red and blue mixed with white will not change the hue. When you pay for a ski lift ticket and count your change, you are using crystallized intelligence. Coming down the hill, responding to the variations of terrain, is a fluid event. In fact, it has been demonstrated that the more fluid intelligence a competitive skier possesses, the more likely is that skier to be successful (Gensemer 1974).

Analytically, one can conclude that most sports performance requires fluid rather than crystallized intelligence. According to Horn and Cattell (1966), who are largely responsible for these concepts, persons with well-formed fluid abilities have a greater capacity to receive perceptual information, organize it conceptually, and respond variably (but appropriately) to the environment. These findings exactly match the demands made of performers in field hockey, or tennis, or football, or lacrosse, or basketball, or almost any other sport. The environment is not static, and neither are the players. A game is a constantly changing, moving, circumstantial thing. In a real sense, it is a *fluid* happening. The ability to respond effectively requires versatility and adaptability—the properties of fluid intelligence.

A content-centered educational setting aims at crystallized intelligence—the teacher tells, the students repeat. Process education attempts to maximize fluid intelligence—the teacher suggests, the students discover. Telling students an exact, undeviating way to serve a tennis ball is content-oriented and appeals to crystallized abilities; allowing students to experiment with various ways of serving the ball is process learning and a utilization of fluid abilities.

At this point, then, a series of conclusions are in order.

INTELLIGENCE CAN BE CONSIDERED FLUID OR CRYSTALLIZED.

Crystallized intelligence is pure knowledge. Fluid intelligence is conceptualization. You can have both. Or you have neither. You can have one without the other. One does not necessarily relate to the other. One does not necessarily influence the other. You can facilitate one, or neither, or both, or one without the other, or one while affecting the other. More significantly, however,

FLUID INTELLIGENCE IS MORE IMPORTANT FOR THE EVENTS OF DAILY LIVING.

Life itself is variable, always changing. Pure information, which is crystallized intelligence, is an essential base for existence. Fluid intelligence is more functional for the dynamic totality of life, and educational settings can be arranged to facilitate this ability. Accordingly:

PROCESS EDUCATION IS AIMED AT STIMULATING FLUID INTELLIGENCE.

It is the promotion of expressiveness, of self-reliance, and of the flexibility to adapt to a changing environment—the qualities so important in the performance of motor skills.

THE EXECUTION OF MOST MOTOR SKILLS IS ESSENTIALLY A FLUID ENDEAVOR.

The accomplishment of any motor performance generally requires that the performer be either versatile, adaptable, or self-expressive. Activities can range from the largely self-generative (as in some forms of dance or free gymnastics) to the more stylized (as in golf or formal gymnastics). In no case, however, is everything static. Situations are always changing. Thus it can be concluded that

PHYSICAL EDUCATION SHOULD BE PROCESS ORIENTED.

Physical education may quite possibly have the greatest potential of all educational endeavors for developing the qualities of fluid intelligence. It is the only discipline which approaches learning from both the mental and the physical domains; resultingly it is a total enterprise.

Physical Performance as Process

Motor performances can generally be thought of as free affairs, distinguishable from "work." We usually do them from free will, voluntarily, because we want to. Often, the reason for participation is the pleasure derived from the activity, and winning may be a secondary concern.

Physical education can provide a preparation for the pleasures which are available in sports participation. Too often, however, the learning may become lost in content concerns. There seems to be a *technique* for the playing of any sport, a proper way to do it. Therefore physical education is professionally involved in showing students the proper ways. The danger is that the very facilitation of motor performance, which is the essence of the profession, can supersede, or completely eliminate, the qualities of the *experience* itself.

Of course, some content is necessary. (Which end of this strange stick do you hit the little ball with?) Not everything can be absolutely experimentive. There just isn't that kind of time. So we need to save students certain frustrations that would assuredly occur if they were left completely to themselves in learning golf, or any other activity. There is always a limit, however, to content; it's too easy to overdo it.

Knowing Too Much

We cannot lose sight of the fact that the great majority of our students (or ourselves, for that matter) do not aspire to physical perfection. Few people are gifted enough to earn a living from physical performance. Contrastingly, most people participate in sports activities as a recreation, or a diversion, or an intrinsic experience. Golf, tennis, jogging, skiing, dance, cycling—all provide a more intensified experience with our own body, bringing mind and body together in a focus not otherwise easily accomplished. These activities offer a *process* in which we can be totally involved—a feeling, a sensation of execution, and a satisfaction in generating our own inpetus. These are moments we can enjoy without the need for winning, or even doing well. It may be that performing for the pure pleasure of it is one of the few remaining human capacities where we can be truly *free*.

Why ruin it? Why not keep it innocent? If we clutter any motor execution with an overabundance of content concerns, we can force the opinion that in order to be enjoyed a performance *must* be done well. And *that* would doom most people to failure, for we are imperfect human beings, vulnerable to motor mistakes. But even though we slice the ball off the first tee, we can still dismiss the world and focus on an experience which is agreeable, sensual, and pleasurable.

We know a great deal today in physical education. We know that the slice comes from certain determined laws of physics. The people who have analyzed those laws of physics, or who have sat in front of video machines watching runners, or who have otherwise studied human motion can provide the necessary information to help us hit the ball straight, or do a sprint with maximal efficiency, or remove a flaw from a dive, or topspin a forehand. It is possible, however, to know so much about a motor execution that we forget about the fact that most students are average, that their idea of activity is enjoyment, not perfection. Physical education must conserve that attitude—not entirely, not exclusively, and not to the point of ignoring the content of learning. But certainly the characteristics of motor execution itself and the abilities of the great majority of students oblige us to attend largely to the *process* of the experiences which physical education can provide.

SOLUTION TO THREE-CUBE PUZZLE: Cube 3 has one dot on the bottom.

CHAPTER 7

Enlivening the Physical

When we were children, we had a natural inclination for physical movement. There was a pure pleasure in it. We used it for feeling free. No one *made* us move. No one showed us *how*. We just did it. In some unexplainable way, we learned more about ourselves by doing it. Could we walk on the fence? Could we jump the stream? How high a tree could we climb?

Movement was us, and we were it. Even before we could speak, we moved and movement was our language. We learned to buy affection with bodily movements; when we wanted to say no to something, our whole body said no. Later, when we saw a bird, we became the bird through movement. When we watched an ant at work, we watched and imitated with our whole body. We learned to count by using our fingers. When we painted a picture, we did it with our body, our brain, our entire self.

Then we went to school and were told to sit quietly all day, watching, listening, being unobtrusive. When 1:40 on Tuesday and Thursday afternoons finally arrived and we went to the gymnasium for physical education, all we wanted to do for five minutes was to run all over the place— just to do it, to let it all out for awhile, to remember that we really still had our physical selves. But we may have been told we were too boisterous.

Over the years we learned to repress our body's impulses. Language took over for physical gestures. We sat motionless while watching movies of birds. We looked at bugs through a microscope and needed only one eye for that. We punched buttons on a calculator for math problems. We were taught to paint using only small hand movements. The body was disappearing. We didn't need it anymore. Even now, when turning on the television, we are reminded of how we can disguise, mask, camouflage, and otherwise ignore our own body. Moreover, any drugstore can provide the pharmacological help needed to subdue a pain, to fall asleep at night, or to wake up in the morning.

The Revival of the Physical

Today, however, there is a renewed interest in the human body. Once again we are attending to the physical self. No longer is there a mind and body separate. We now recognize that mental and physical events are interrelated, dependent on each other, influencing each other. Quite clearly, we are one whole, complete person.

The ancient Greeks told us this truth long ago; we have only recently rediscovered it. Eastern philosophy has provided some help. Zen is now used on tennis courts, on ski slopes, and on golf courses. Additionally, the popularity of books on "body language" has made society aware that we are, in fact, overt actors of inner states of emotion. The intriguing study of biofeedback has made it clear that the mind can exert control over physiological states once thought to be involuntary (Brown 1977). There is little question today, then, about the distinct and close linkage between mind and body.

A Responsive Answer to a Responsive Matter

Intriguingly, physical education has a process available to it whereby the mind/body harmony can be heightened. It is a process usually called *movement education*. Sometimes it may be called movement exploration, or basic movement, or just plain movement, or educational gymnastics. The most accurate term, however, is movement education, and it means just that—movement and education.It is not simply a technique for the education *of* movement; rather, it also includes the very important concept of education *through* movement.

In essence, movement education is a means of using a physical medium for becoming one's own best self. It is an enhancement of the total being—firstly of the body and its capabilities, and secondly of the psyche, with the body as its expression. In its most complete application, it develops a conscious receptiveness to the proprioceptive impulses that arise from movement and then generates an ability to utilize that information for the effective control of muscular activity. The effect is to increase the communication between the mind and the body, with positive influences on both.

Specifically, movement education attempts to provide—

1. An educational environment of freedom, with a correlated encouragement for students to use the physical self as a means of expressing states of mind.
2. Experiences specifically designed to increase the conscious awareness of the proprioceptive sensations that arise from within the physical self.
3. An educational arrangement which will promote an increased ability to execute purposeful, effective, and skillful motor responses.

It was first thought (and is still, unfortunately, believed by many) that the technique of movement education was suitable only for children. The original contentions were that by providing the freedom to run and climb and jump and explore and discover and create, children would somehow, osmotically, become more perceptive and creative individuals. Some did, of course, but they probably would have become so without the freedom. For most, however, the conceptual and creative stages never arrived, and important learning years were spent running and climbing and jumping.

Today the concerns of movement education are more than a mere "allowance" for physical expression. Understandably, an atmosphere of movement freedom *is* a part of the method, but only as the starting point. The technique is actually designed to *use* movement freedom as an experimentive self-discovery process of motor skill learning. Most appealing of all is the fact that the method can be used for *all* students, regardless of ability, previous experience, or age.

The Foundation of the Method

In its most fundamental form

THE METHOD OF MOVEMENT EDUCATION IS BASED ON THE TWO PRINCIPLES OF EXPLORATION AND PROBLEM SOLVING.

In application, the teacher normally offers students a "problem" which requires that they respond with a motoric answer. To arrive at the answers, students are encouraged to use exploratory behavior, trying one response after another until the most effective answers are self-discovered. Accordingly, the teacher does not demonstrate movements and expect students to mimic them; rather, the teacher acts as a catalyst to stimulate the students' use of motoric experimentation for their own solving of the problems. The intent is to encourage self-initiated trial-and-error motor behavior and the self-appropriated learning of the most efficient uses of movement.

Always, the learning experiences begin with a free allowance for experimentation; they evolve into teacher-suggested responses as needed. For example, a teacher may introduce a learning unit in volleyball by simply allowing students to experiment with different ways to keep the ball in the air. Then, the teacher begins to make suggestions to students, in effect presenting a series of problems, such as "Discover the parts of your hand that you can use to keep the ball in the air," or "Is there one best way to control the ball?" or "What do you need to do to receive a ball and keep it in play without catching it?"

The encouraged movement responses in any learning situation are never expected to be picturebook in form. Often, there is no single correct response. Individualism is always recognized and is in fact promoted. Exploration remains a constant in the method; but in the "art" of the method, the teacher is expected to *direct* the explorations toward predetermined objectives. The degree of direction depends primarily on the nature of the subject being taught. Modern dance, for instance, requires less specific direction than golf. Always, however, the spirit of the exploratory allowance is maintained.

To illustrate the versatility of this method, two examples follow. One presents a situation where the teacher encourages the free experimentation and learning of generalized movement with children; the other uses the same technique to teach a tennis forehand. In the first situation, using no equipment, the teacher merely gives the children an open space. The suggestions from the teacher may be like those in the first example.

1. Move around the room in any way that you like.
2. See if you can move quietly.
3. Can you find more than one way to move on your feet, not just running?
4. Be as heavy as you can while you move; now as light as you can. Can you be very low? How about very wide?
5. When I clap my hands, freeze into a position.
6. Now, make a turning motion as you move around the room.
7. Move any way that you like, now, and try to stay as far away from everyone else as you can as you move around. Now, move very fast, still staying far away from everyone else.
8. Find a space on the floor away from everyone else.
9. See how many different ways you can support your body on the floor. Try different parts—not just standing or sitting.
10. Use four parts of your body to support your weight; now, three; now, two; now, one; now, a different one; and, now, a different two.
11. Find a partner, and see if you can help your partner to achieve a balance that could not otherwise be achieved alone.
12. Can the two of you find a balance position in which both of you are dependent on each other for that balance? Can you move that position around, high and low, and in a circle?
13. Now, you and your partner find a way to keep your balance steady while trying to pull away from each other. Can you find more than one way to do this?
14. Now, let's move around the room again. This time see if you can change from moving very quickly to moving very slowly, then back to moving quickly again, as often as you like.
15. Can you change from being very strong in your movement to being very weak and back again?

In the tennis class, the conversation may be something like the following:

TEACHER:	You've all had an opportuniy to experiment with your forehand for the last fifteen minutes. What are some of the things you learned?
HARRY:	Well, I found out that if you swing upward, the ball goes over the fence.
ANNETTA:	Me, too. I kept hitting the ball too far, but then I could change it and make the ball go into the court.
TEACHER	How did you make that change?
ANNETTA:	Well, ah—I'm not sure, really. I just sort of swung the racket differently.
TEACHER:	Actually, you're describing one of the basics of an effective forehand. Does anyone know what I mean?
DONALD:	I think you mean you can hit the ball wherever you want it to go by changing your swing.

TEACHER: Yes, exactly. It means, mostly, that the ball will go in the direction you are swinging. If you swing up, the ball will normally go up, and if you swing down, that's where it will go. There are some exceptions, as we'll see when we experiment with changes in the angle of the racket face. But essentially the ball goes in the direction of the swing. Now, is there is anything we can do to help us in this respect?

HELEN: I don't think I know what you mean.

TEACHER: Well, is there anything we can do with our body during the swing to help the ball go in the direction we want it to go?

BOB: We can turn it.

TEACHER: That's true. But what is happening at the very moment that you hit the ball? How is the body moving?

CONNIE: I'm not sure this is right, but do you mean we have stepped into the ball?

TEACHER: In a way, yes. I'm glad you said that, because that's what most of the books on tennis say that you should do. But if we want the ball to go in that direction, how can we step to help us hit it that way?

ANNETTA: Oh, I see what you mean. We should step toward the net or—I mean, toward where we want the ball to go.

TEACHER: You're exactly right. That's good. What it really means is that our feeling of body momentum should be such that we are moving in the direction we want to hit the ball at the time we make contact. We can help ourselves by stepping not so much "into" the ball, but more toward the spot that we want to hit the ball. Do you suppose this will also help our swing?

HARRY: It seems as if it would help the swing to go in that direction.

TEACHER: Indeed it does. So now you have two of the most important principles in hitting a good forehand. They are that both the swing and the body movement should be going in the direction you want to hit the ball at the moment you make contact. Sometimes, of course, we are on the run and it isn't so easy to do this, but when the ball gives us enough time to collect ourselves before we hit, we should try to do both. Now I'd like you to hit some more forehands, and as you do, try to *sense* that all your impulses are going in the direction you want the ball to go as you make your hit.

Although the second of these two scenarios is not movement education in the classical sense, the underlying principles of experimentation and problem solving remain. In this way, the students become responsible for their own learning, as the teacher becomes the stimulus but not the dictator of their discoveries.

All Problems Have Answers

In the most literal sense, a "problem" is a situation which is proposed for consideration or solution. Generally, the implicaion is that there *is* a solution. However, in the presentation to students of an open-ended suggestion to "Move on the balance beam in any way that you like," or similar statement, there is no real solution. Instead, there is only the doing.

But as the educational objectives become more specific, the pure exploration of this method becomes replaced by what Mosston (1966) has called "guided discovery." This is a nonstructured technique whereby the teacher narrows the range of potential responses to a problem by giving students verbal suggestions to guide their experimentation. Never does the teacher actually *tell* students how to respond, instead the guidance remains only *suggestive*. In this way the *process* of education is preserved, for the students have the freedom necessary to invent and experiment, and the teacher's function is to encourage self-appropriated learnings.

This technique has wide application. Generally, it *begins* with exploration and then *evolves* into guided discovery. No matter what the learning unit, the age of the learners, or their abilities, the method always includes the following sequence:

THE INITIAL LEARNING EXPERIENCES ARE PROVIDED AS AN OPEN ALLOWANCE FOR AND AN ENCOURAGEMENT OF UNSTRUCTURED EXPLORATION.

Thus a teacher may begin a unit in soccer by offering such suggestions as "Move the ball around the field in any way that you like," and "Try to use as many different body parts as you can to move the ball." Then, as the learning sequence progresses, it begins more and more to take on the characteristics of guided discovery. Thus:

THE FACILITATION OF LEARNING IS PROVIDED THROUGH PROBLEM-SOLVING EXPERIENCES.

And:

STUDENTS ARE ASSISTED IN THE PROBLEM-SOLVING EXPERIENCES BY THE GUIDED SUGGESTIONS OF THE TEACHER.

In the soccer unit, the teacher may next say, "How can you move the ball without using your hands?" or "Can you move the ball while keeping it on the ground?" or "Is there a part of your foot which can best keep the ball under control?" Since this guided discovery technique is comparatively unstructured,

THE PROCESS OF MOTOR EXPERIMENTATION IS THE MEDIUM OF LEARNING.

With some skill learning, there may be only a small range of effective responses; consequently teacher guidance needs to be relatively specific. In other instances where the activity permits a wide range of answers, the guidance may be more of an encouragement for the purity of exploration.

Being Willing to Do Nothing

In movement education, the *product* of the experiences is not the dominating factor. Rather, it is believed that by giving the responsibility for the learning to students (instead of to the teacher), the *process* of their involvement in self-discovery is also an educational experience. Not only do students learn, but they "learn about learning," which requires of the teacher the patience to await responses which may often seem slow in occurring. Since the method provides students the freedom to generate their own responses, the process is very individual. Resultingly, students will need sufficient time to arrive at the solutions at their own rate.

This requirement for individual time allowances is based on the personalized nature of problem-solving activities. Before anyone can respond to a problem-solving situation, a period of cognitive organization—a time for "thinking through" the problem—is necessary. Depending on the difficulty of the problem, this period may be an interval in which absolutely nothing appears to be happening. In this event some psychological stress may be placed on a teacher who interprets the inactivity as a state of "nothingness" and reacts by offering preliminary clues to the solution. In fact, such assistance may only confuse the original problem (Stein 1975). It appears that there *must* be an interval in which students are allowed the freewheeling information processing which is an essential start to solving problems (Newell and Simon 1972). This preliminary brainstorming is an organizational process which varies widely from individual to individual (Scandura 1977).

Further, the second stage of problem solving is experimentation. Not only is it necessary to allow time for cognitive processing, it is also imperative that the first responses be completely trial and error and that no help be given during this time (Maltzman 1960). The introduction of guided assistance, which should be added to the learning experience at about the time frustration begins to plague a student, then becomes a matter of teacher judgment (Schmuck, Chesler, and Lippitt 1966).

Finally, teacher assistance must consist of open-ended suggestions, never a mere providing of answers; for the problem-solving experience will be effective only if it culminates in personal self-operation on the situation and a self-discovered answer (Rickards 1974).

The moral here is that the teacher can ruin it all by teaching. Certainly, any person professionally employed as a teacher feels a natural inclination to help students learn. The humanistic ideal of providing freedom for learning, however, does *not* imply any attempt to *make* students learn. Instead, it conveys an *allowance* for learning. In problem-solving endeavors this means providing the time individually needed by each student to arrive at solutions. In this sense, then, doing nothing is actually doing something, and oververbalization at this critical time may be one of the most hindering factors in the learning process (Marteniuk 1976).

The Inside Story

Traditional teaching methods place a reliance on outside sources (teachers, books, tests) for the gathering of information. In movement education the sources are mostly internal.Holistically, this may be the greatest service to learners that the attitude engendered by movement education can give.

The psychological freedom which is the necessary starting point for problem-solving endeavors will automatically turn students to themselves. The intellectual freedom provided through teacher suggestions will also generate internalizations of learning. Moreover, the movement freedom which accompanies the method is a means of focusing on impulses which are entirely internal. Interestingly, the last of these freedoms may have a neurological reality.

As humanism can free the mind, so can the method of movement education free the body. First the mind must be *relieved* of any constraints by providing psychological and intellectual freedom, which in turn *alerts* the mind to what the body is saying.

This is a kind of biofeedback. Broadly seen, biofeedback is a return of some input from an output; that is, any action of the body sets off nerve impulses which are a result of that action. All actions are informative: when we stub a toe there is feedback; when we add too much hot sauce to a taco there is feedback; when we take a golf club into the backswing there is feedback. What this revolutionary technique does is to teach persons to listen to their internal sources of information and then use them as guides for the *control* of internal affairs. In essence, when we learn to monitor our internal proprioceptive information, we become more acquainted with our inner selves, and with practice we can exert conscious influence on physiological states through a sort of mind-over-matter process.

Probably, the technique originated with Jacobson (1962), who has used it to teach countless numbers of persons self-relaxation. This method alerts people to the *differences* in their muscular sensations. Not only are they asked to focus on their proprioceptive impulses, they are also taught to perceive and then to create changes in muscular states. The deceptively simple method of this technique requests the person to tighten a particular muscle group as hard as possible and then focus on the sensation arising from the tension. Next, the muscle group is allowed to completely relax, and the mind is attentive to the new and different sensation in the muscles. Then, the muscle group is tightened half as hard as previously, and the attention is again given to the feedback coming from that state. The theory underlying this awareness is that if the brain learns to recognize physiological states of relaxation, it can then create them.

It's legitimate. This internal feedback system provides information for the self-recognition of something often referred to in the psychological literature as "just noticeable differences." Specifically this is the ability of a person to perceive small differences in sensory feedback. As an example, suppose you went to the grocery store and picked up ten pounds of sugar. But wait—that sack felt too light. Sure enough there's a hole in it and some sugar has spilled out. Pick up another one—this one is all right. Now, then, how much sugar had to spill out of the first sack before you could test its weight and know, by comparing it with the other, whether it is lighter in weight. An ounce? A few ounces? A full pound? In fact, almost all persons can recognize a ten percent difference between two different stimuli. Therefore, almost all persons can sense the difference between ten pounds and nine pounds. Not so many persons, however, can recognize a difference of just a few ounces. This same neurological functioning permits one golfer to shoot in the 70s and keeps another forever over 100. No golfer can really *watch* the club when swinging it. It is therefore necessary to rely on the information which is generated proprioceptively. The muscular system, then, uses its own feedback system to guide the finite movements required for effective golf play. Quite obviously, some persons are given a more refined feedback system than others.

Discouragingly, we can do very little to alter the particular efficiency of the system we happen to be born with (Singer 1975); but, encouragingly, we can learn to *use* what we have more effectively. Both the Jacobson relaxation technique and biofeedback use this same principle. It's a matter of *tuning in* to the sensations that are there, a matter of changing the *attentiveness* from a dependent reliance on external sources (including teachers) and giving it instead to the internal proprioceptive sensations. This is also the philosophy and method of movement education.

The Dimensions of Inner Space

Rudolph Laban, the originator of movement education, started it all. His writings consistently emphasized certain differential qualities which distinguish human movement: space, weight, time, and flow (see especially Laban 1947 and 1948). The meaning of these qualities is not so important as the fact of their existence. Collectively they remind us that movement and its control are a multidimensional affair. There are differences in speed, intensity, pace, rhythm, tension, and everything else. In Laban's opinion a movement education program must provide experiences which will alert the participants to these dimensions of human action, with the final consequence of increasing the ability to make minor adjustments in their execution.

The relationship between these movement qualities and the internal feedback system can be developed when the teacher of young children suggests that they "Find a different way to move in a space" or when the high school teacher asks the golf class to "Change to more of an inside-out swing and see what the effect is." Such teaching attempts to change the student's usual ways of perceiving. When artfully administered, the final product is a biofeedback kind of learning which is available to each student.

The Choreography of the Methodology

In summary, by using the technique of movement education at *all* levels of learning, the teacher—

- Provides a three-dimensional freedom: *psychological freedom* to establish the foundational atmosphere; *intellectual freedom* to be encouraged by guided discovery; and *movement freedom* to enable students to recognize that they are not performing to imitate some preestablished motor patterns as the only acceptable responses.

- Allows an initial time in a new learning for student exploration. During this time there should be no actual instruction, only the permission for an unstructured trial-and-error motor experimentation.
- Introduces "problems" specifically designed to direct student experimentation toward predetermined objectives. These problems must be presented in open-ended fashion, with the teacher offering suggestions but never providing answers to the "solutions."In this way, the method always allows the appropriate responses to be self-discovered by students.
- Consciously directs the final attention of students to their internal feedback systems. The curtain call of the movement education method comes when students can leave the educational setting and take with them the perceptual abilities that were always within them but were generally unused. This is the art of the art. In a very realistic sense, the more effective this endeavor becomes, the more students evolve into their own best critics. This is humanism's finest hour, for the internalization is not only psychological, it is also physiological—an educational experience which deals with the *whole person*.

The Bottom Half of the Ninth

It would be unrealistic to deny that humanism is founded on a great deal of common sense. It would by myopic to ignore its importance for physical education. In an educational endeavor as fluid, as personalized, and as internal as physical education, humanism offers a great deal of logic. But before we add up the final score, we must allow behaviorism to have its time at bat.

CHAPTER 8

An Emergent Style of Learning

Ivan Petrovich Pavlov may have started the whole affair by such an innocuous thing as giving meaning to saliva. He had watched his hungry dogs salivate every time they heard a bell which signified that food was on its way. Was something in the mind controlling something physiological? For four years he had asked himself that question; and when he had finished, the world of physiologists, psychiatrists, and psychologists was standing at attention. From these craving canines came the new concepts of inhibition, extinction, and, most importantly, the conditioned (and *controllable*) reflex.

Then there was, and still is, Burrhus Frederick Skinner whose experiments showed, in effect, that not only can you lead a horse to water, but you can make the horse drink—by using something called reinforcement. Skinner first became aware of this phenomenon by observing pigeons—in a box. In this container called, however rhetorically, a Skinner box, he coerced unwilling pigeons into performing certain predetermined behaviors for the reward of food. With this little device, hundreds of experiments produced mountains of data on the effects of reinforcement (Skinner 1959). In a less serious mood, Skinner once taught pigeons to play ping-pong. The significant fact, however, is that he eventually found the same principles to work on human beings. Ultimately his scheme, which he called operant conditioning, became the most widely used behavioral management technique that education has ever employed.

Finally, there is the family in Oconomowoc, Wisconsin, whose three-year-old son, Ronnie, will not eat. Although his parents have offered him every kind of food, Ronnie refuses it all. Refusing Ronnie. Mealtimes have become a problem. His mother believes there must be something physically wrong with the boy, and she is sympathetic. His father just gets angry. At other times, both parents simply ignore Ronnie. They have too many things to do—dad is involved with his profession and mom with the housework. But when Ronnie is eating, or more accurately not eating, they give him attention—both sympathy and anger, but attention. It is a scene played daily, by the thousands, in homes all over the country.

Each of these illustrations has a common element—behavioral control. Pavlov was able to induce salivation in dogs through the use of a previously unrelated stimulus. Skinner used pellets of food to produce certain responses in pigeons. And Ronnie receives some usually absent attention by refusing to eat. In each case, a behavior was influenced by the way the environment reacted to that behavior. Because of the environmental reaction (the giving of food or attention), the chances are increased that the same behavior will occur again in the future, under the same circumstances. Ronnie, for example, will probably continue his refusing behavior as long as his parents give him attention (the environmental reaction) for not eating. The immediate response of the environment has, therefore, influenced future behavior.

There it is—the surprisingly simple ground floor of behavioral psychology. In a few words:

BEHAVIOR IS AFFECTED BY ITS CONSEQUENCES. THE FUTURE OCCURENCE OF ALL BEHAVIORS IS INFLUENCED BY THE WAY IN WHICH THE ENVIRONMENT (WHICH USUALLY MEANS PEOPLE) RESPONDS TO THOSE BEHAVIORS.

Direct, genuine, and candid. So unadulterated that even Skinner himself, considered the quarterback of the behaviorists, admitted that the basic principle was so simple it was embarrassing (Skinner 1966b).

If there is any art in behavioral science, it lies in its simplicity. It is amazingly forthright, eliminating anything unnecessary. All programs of behavior modification are based on this single, most important premise.

Imagine a father in Hoxie, Kansas, absorbed in the weekly autumn ritual of watching Monday night football when his two-year-old son asks for a piece of candy. "No, not now, candy isn't any good for you," says dad. The son begins to cry—just a whimper at first, but loud enough to disturb his father. "Quiet, son. I can't hear," implores dad. "Want candy!" pleads the boy, beginning to cry louder. "Wait till your mother gets home; she'll get you some," dad snaps. Then the crying becomes even louder. "All right, all right!" says dad, quickly finding a piece of candy, which he gives his son who predictably stops crying. The not-so-naive two-year-old son realizes that if he cries again he will probably get another piece of candy. He is gaining control.

In Punxsutawney, Pennsylvania, there is a very autocratic, unsympathetic physical education teacher whose students dislike his classes. Rick, who can't tolerate it anymore, decides to create a disturbance, shoving a couple of other students around and throwing a basketball against the wall. As a result he is dismissed from class and is sent to the school disciplinarian. That's not so bad; it's better than the class. Rick knew he would get tossed out of class by causing a disruption, and he'll probably do it again. It is Rick, not the teacher, who is controlling the behavior.

A piece of candy is pleasurable. A certain class may be aversive. By crying the two-year-old was able to obtain candy. By disruptive behavior Rick was able to avoid the class. Therein lies the second important principle of behaviorism:

PEOPLE WILL TRY TO ACHIEVE SITUATIONS THEY FIND PLEASURABLE AND TO AVOID SITUATIONS THEY FIND AVERSIVE.

In effect, it says that we do what we like and we don't do what we don't like. Crying was a behavior that *achieved* a pleasurable state; disruptive behavior *avoided* something aversive.

A whole science of human management has been built on these two very direct and obvious principles. These principles contain nothing provocative. It is not their uniqueness that has made behavior modification effective. Rather, it is the reliability of their occurrence which has led to the widespread utilization of behaviorism in contemporary education.

Laws Are for Things and Laws Are for People

Certain laws in the physical world cannot be violated. Apples always fall downward. When you step into a completely filled bathtub, some water will spill over. A billiard ball responds in direct opposition to the force of another ball striking it. As complex as it is, human behavior also appears to follow certain basic laws. Countless numbers of rats, dogs, and pigeons have given early evidence. And more recent observations of human beings have verified the contention that people do indeed respond in highly predictable ways to specific environmental happenings. When the principles by which human behavior operates are known, it becomes possible to effect changes in the future behaviors of people, or to modify behavior.

Nothing New

The techniques now used in behavior modification have been known for some time. The principles were first formally documented in writing in 1800 (Verhave 1966). Some early controlled research was accomplished in the mid-1800s (Williams and Long 1975), and John B. Watson (1920) clearly outlined the foundations decades ago. Still, it did not really become a stronghold in education until the 1960s. Since then, behavior modification has been successfully employed in an astounding variety of circumstances. The following are some examples of its use in altering the behaviors of younger school children:

Reducing hyperactivity
Increasing physical activity
Eliminating children's rejection of adults
Reducing children's dependency on adults
Promoting social interaction with other children
Producing increased verbal competence
Eliminating excessive crying
Eliminating isolated play habits
Reducing disruptive behavior in class
Eliminating noncooperative behavior
Increasing attention span and reading performance
Producing creative writing skills
Promoting conceptual understandings and memory
Increasing mathematical performance

Increasing spelling competence
Eliminating letter and word reversals
Encouraging interest in physical skill development

(Further examples may be found in Klein, Hapkiewicz, and Roden 1973.)

No magical secrets are used to effect these changes—just pure and basic behavioristic principles. For teachers, the best part is that even though behavior modification is part of a highly technical system based on organized laboratory research investigation, its application is not difficult to learn and to use. No exotic technique is necessary, nor does one need long experience. The only requirements are to translate the laboratory experiments and written words into action, and to interact with others.

CHAPTER 9

The Qualification of Behavior

Behavior, by itself, may literally refer to anything a person does. In behavioristic terms, however, it is never used in such a broad sense as in the sentence, "Randy is behaving today," or in the question,"How did your class behave?" More accurately, it means any human response of *observable* and *measurable* activity. Driving a car is a behavior that is easily observed and measurable by distance traveled, speed at any moment, and so forth. Bowling is a similar type of activity. In this regard, behavior is what people are doing, what can be seen as their activity, an *observable* product. It is not an attitude, nor a state of mind, nor a feeling. In a gymnastics class students might be *seen* to exhibit the general behaviors of bouncing on a trampoline, doing a mount on the parallel bars, swinging on the high bar, spotting, just standing idly—all of which are overtly observable activities. Behaviors do not tell us how students may *feel* about the class, however, only what they are *doing*.

What You See Is What You Get

The criterion by which all behavioristic schemes are tested is *observable behavior*. It is the real indicator of success and the only valid means of judging the outcomes of teaching. Therefore:

A BEHAVIOR IS IMPORTANT ONLY IF IT CAN BE OBSERVED.

Some behaviors are easily observed, others more difficult. For instance, the next time you have an activity class, observe some of the things students are doing. In a soccer class, for example, some students may be seen shooting at the goal, another playing goalkeeper, some practicing dribbling, a few doing heading, some just fooling around. Such behaviors are fairly easy to observe, since they are overt and clear evidences of what is happening. But if you were to ascertain the behaviors of students in a classroom setting, it might be more difficult to determine exactly what they were doing. In this situation the behaviors are more subtle. As an example, at your next opportunity, observe students in a classroom and mark down the number you see doing the following:

———— Listening to the teacher
———— Thinking about what the teacher is saying
———— Daydreaming
———— Taking notes
———— Doing work for another class

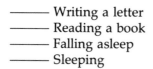

———— Writing a letter
———— Reading a book
———— Falling asleep
———— Sleeping

A little trial such as this can indicate the difficulty of categorizing human behavior. How can you know if students are listening to the teacher? By their attentiveness? By their watching the teacher? They may be daydreaming instead, whereas someone staring out the window who appears to be daydreaming may be listening to the teacher. Moreover, someone who is thinking very intently about the content of what the teacher is saying may appear to be sleeping. In these cases you can record only what you can *see*—in overt behaviors. Perhaps all that can be said about a particular classroom is that three students are "sitting quietly." That may be the only behavior which is apparent. And unless we can come up with some very definable way of knowing the specific behaviors which are evidences of such vague terms as thinking, listening, and day-dreaming, we can speak only of the *outward* behaviors of students.

Another blurred concept is this thing called attitude. How do you measure it? By itself, attitude is not a behavior because it cannot be directly observed. Therefore, it cannot be measured. Since it cannot be measured, it is not important. Yet attitude may be a component of physical education teachers' evaluations of students.

It may of course be a surface deduction, for certain behaviors are overt reflections of student attitudes. But it is not enough to say, for example, that a student has a "negative attitude" about school. Instead, it is necessary to find evidence in such acts as frequent truancy, failure to turn in assignments, creating class disturbances, verbal statements made by the student, and so on. Otherwise, according to behavioristic standards, any conclusions made about a student's attitude are invalid.

This illustration indicates the difficulty of describing human behavior by using only hypothetical constructs. Attitudes, feelings, and emotions by themselves are not behaviors, although certain behaviors may be considered *evidences* of those concepts. One cannot measure what one cannot see, however, and one cannot see a feeling. In the realm of behaviorism, then:

BEHAVIOR IS AN OBSERVABLE AND MEASURABLE ACT OF A PERSON. BEHAVIOR IS WHAT PEOPLE OVERTLY DO, AND ONLY WHAT PEOPLE OVERTLY DO IS IMPORTANT.

In effect, then, to judge the effectiveness of any teaching, it is necessary to observe the overt products evidenced in student behaviors.

Observable Behavior Qualifies Teacher Effectiveness

Much human behavior can easily be recorded—heart rate, blood pressure, brain waves, golf score, number of situps. Suppose, however, a teacher said to you, "Jeff is a troublemaker." Your retort might be, "How do you know?" The teacher might reply, "Just look at the way he behaves." And the question might then be, "But exactly what behaviors give you the opinion that he is indeed a troublemaker?"

Behavior is often stated in hypothetical terms, and conclusions are frequently hypothetical. For example, an objective of physical education may include the statement "to meet the needs of students." But exactly what *are* those needs? How can they be defined? What are the observable evidences of those needs?

Further, how do you define some other recurring objectives such as "cooperative play," or "competitive spirit," or "respect for the rules," or "appreciation of the game," or "leadership"? These concepts exist as standards in the profession; yet if any teaching efforts actually accomplish these ends, it is largely unknown for the concepts themselves are difficult to define. Thus it is not easy to decide on the behavioral components of the concepts; and therefore the evidences cannot be seen. Since they cannot be seen, they cannot be measured; and since they cannot be measured, they cannot be evaluated; and since they cannot be evaluated, they are not important.

Accordingly, when a human trait cannot be defined in observable behavioral components, that trait cannot be included as a legitimate educational endeavor. The evaluation of teaching effectiveness therefore becomes extremely difficult to determine when the objectives are stated in nonbehavioral concepts. This statement does not deny that such components may in fact exist. Rather, it emphasizes the importance of determining the evidences of their existence.

As a critical example, one of the main objectives and purported outcomes of humanistic teaching is the development of creativity. What *is* creativity? Can it be defined as a feeling? an expression? a process? an inner happening? By behavioristic standards, it must be definable through observable and measurable products. To exemplify the difficulty, list some of the behaviors you believe are *evidences* of creativity.

If you mentioned such traits as flexibility, originality, expressiveness, or spontaneity, then you listed some of the commonly accepted coinage often used to describe creativity. The words themselves, however, are also open to varied interpretation. Flexibility can be an inner trait, shown by the ability to generate diverse solutions to the same problem, or it can be an external trait, reflected by an ability to adapt to new situations. Originality is a factor specific to each individual; that is, what is original thought or behavior to one person may be old hat to another. Expressiveness may be the exemplification of frustration rather than any creative impetus, and spontaneity may be a product of disorganized thinking rather than of abstract abilities.

Behaviorism requires that creativity be given a more specific and definite description. To this end, we might (emphasis on the "might") then arrive at some conclusions which resemble the following:

Creativity is—1. Causing something to come into existence for the first time.
2. Arranging things in novel ways.

72

3. Originating a new idea.
4. Conceiving of solutions to abstract problems.
5. Exploring available equipment and showing new movement patterns on that equipment.
6. Joining together elements that are customarily thought of as separate and dissimilar.
7. Forming new combinations of associative elements which are in some way useful.

Even these definitions are vulnerable to speculation and interpretation as diverse as the people reading them. Creativity may be one of those amorphous human aptitudes that simply cannot be defined. Jones (1972) thought so, for after a thorough literature search for an approvable definition, he was led to conclude that "The process of creativity is so complex that to define it too precisely might do it a disservice" (p. 7). Skinner (1968) agreed, but he also emphatically stressed the necessity for an attempt at some sort of behavioral definition. Whatever it is, said Skinner, creativity probably *does* exist, somewhere; but until it can be defined it must remain outside the objectives of behavioristic education, for until we know exactly what it *is*, we cannot know what to look for as behavioral evidence of its presence, and so we cannot know what to *teach for*.

Defining Behavior Provides Directions for Teaching

This concern with definitions may seem a bit exaggerated, but such sensitivity in describing human conduct will become extremely useful when we begin to consider the specific characteristics of motor skills. As a reward for this meticulous scrutiny, we will be given specific cues about the teaching of those skills. Further, the more exact one is in this endeavor, the more guidance it provides. In addition, communication problems will be reduced. Students and teachers will begin to understand each other more easily because they will have a defined set of objectives, a means of attaining those objectives, and a method for evaluating progress. All depends on the human capacity for precision.

This specific, behavioristic approach to teaching leaves no room for some of the more universally accepted but indistinct objectives of physical education. For example, how do you now define the two following standards which purportedly occur from participation in physical education—emotional stability and cooperative play?

This is more than an exercise in semantics. While it is understandably difficult to describe and evaluate many behaviors thought to accrue from physical education, it is nonetheless important at least to attempt definitions. This practice will encourage an attitude of careful observation of human behavior. It will remind teachers of exactly what they are trying to teach, what they must look for in their students, and what their students must do to show that they are learning. If teaching is ever to enter the realm of science, it will happen only when there is a thorough acceptance of the behavioristic attitude.

Knowing What to Look For

Assume that you have a swimming class where the lesson is on the crawl stroke. You have a list of the following behaviors to observe in students:

1. Showing fear of the water
2. Thinking about doing the crawl stroke
3. Doing the crawl stroke
4. Learning by watching others doing the crawl stroke
5. Listening to verbalizations about the crawl stroke
6. Thinking about how neat someone else looks in a swimming suit
7. Wishing the water was warmer
8. Wishing they were somewhere else

Of the eight behaviors, which are more clearly observable? Probably only the third. The others may all be happening, but until we have defined their observable consequences, we cannot definitely conclude that we see evidences of their existence. Thus:

DEFINING BEHAVIOR IS THE FIRST STEP TOWARD CHANGING BEHAVIOR.

The first requirement for eliciting positive changes in people's behavior is to objectify the behaviors to be effected. This is simply a precision required of any science, and behavior modification can literally be considered a "science" of education.

Nothing Is Permanent

According to behaviorism, there is no behavior that cannot be changed provided it has been carefully defined.

ANY BEHAVIOR CAN BE CHANGED AS LONG AS IT CAN BE STATED IN OBSERVABLE TERMS.

This is a critical item in the behavior modification format. Were all behavior not subject to influence from outside sources, then all concern about specificity in defining the components of human acts would be meaningless. Of course, then, it follows that:

BEHAVIOR CAN MOST EFFECTIVELY BE CHANGED THROUGH THE SYSTEMATIC APPLICATION OF THE METHODS OF BEHAVIORAL SCIENCE.

This means that not only are all behaviors open to change, but there is a best way to make the change. By pairing behaviors with their known consequences, it becomes possible to increase, reduce, maintain, restrict, or eliminate selected behaviors. All that is necessary is to control the consequences of people's actions in order to influence the future occurrence of their behaviors. This is a return to the basic principle of the science—people will try to gain pleasurable states and to avoid discomforting ones.

What may be most meaningful of all is that the use of behavioral technology makes it possible to select certain behaviors for alteration while leaving others unaffected. This selection can be made at will, at the discretion of the teacher. One can elect to have students do more math, or increase their reading speed, or complete more projects, or develop a more effective tennis serve. Or one can choose goals that are not specifically academic, such as having students sit in their seats more often, or raise their hands before asking questions, or follow directions more accurately, or work independently, or be attentive to roll call, or eliminate disruptive actions. In addition, teachers who wish to do so may purposefully change their own behavior—to become more organized, or to give more attention to slow learners, or to be less negative, or to smile more frequently.

The behaviorist approach to learning also implies that behavior is subject to varying *degrees* of change. For example, the teacher may wish to effect changes such as the following:

Increase self-directed practice of motor skills.
Reduce aggressive play during a touch football game.
Maintain teamwork among players on a basketball team.
Restrict student talking to times when the teacher is not presenting a
    lesson.
Eliminate periods of class time when students do nothing.

In a physical education class we may find one teacher who is managing student responses with the objective of executing a perfect forward roll, while another is trying to increase student experimentation with tumbling maneuvers. The science of behavior modification will not question which one is right; it will provide the means for each teacher to accomplish individual objectives. This is because the concern of behaviorism does not lie in the particular behaviors to be changed but in the technique that can be used to make the changes.

CHAPTER 10

The Most Influential Strategy: Positive Teaching

Most of us never really think too much about our daily interaction with the environment. We just go through routines subconsciously. We put a key into the ignition of our car to start it. We drop a few coins into a vending machine for a can of soda. We turn on the microwave for a quick supper.

But suppose some of these automatic associations suddenly do not produce the expected results? Our behavior under these new conditions will change. Now we may need to call a mechanic, or kick the vending machine, or cook the meal on top of the old gas burner. Further, if we buy a certain product and do not like it, we'll try another brand next time; if we go to a restaurant and the food is awful, we'll not go back; and if we see a certain type movie and find it absurd, we may not want to see another of the same kind. When we don't get what we want, we are not inclined to repeat the behavior.

Behavioral Consequences

It's all very direct and connecting. We know we can normally depend on the environment to provide certain results for our actions. If the environment fails us, however, we will probably change our actions in the future. Our behaviors are quite literally governed by the consequences of our actions.

So enters the principle of *reinforcement*.

In those situations where the consequences of our actions will strengthen our behavior (that is, make it more likely to occur in similar future situations), the consequences themselves can be considered to provide reinforcement. This is sometimes thought of as a "reward" system. In circumstances where the consequences of our actions make a particular behavior less likely to occur in the future, the consequences can be considered in a broad sense a punisher. If a behavior results in pleasure (or at least in an expected outcome), we will probably repeat that behavior. If, on the other hand, action results in displeasure, we are less likely to repeat it.

The Most Powerful Factor in Behavioristic Teaching

In its broadest interpretation, reinforcement refers to anything which may influence the future occurrence of behaviors. It is the most meaningful function of the application of the science of behavior modification.

Through its use, the teacher is able to arrange the environmental conditions which will result in selected behavioral outcomes. Thus:

THE USE OF REINFORCEMENT IS A PROCEDURE WHICH CAN INCREASE, MAINTAIN, OR REDUCE SELECTED BEHAVIORS.

Reinforcement can be thought of as providing people with pleasurable states as a kind of reward for something they have done. Conversely, it can also administer an unpleasurable state for something they may have done.

In application, reinforcement makes human behavior controllable. It is the ammunition of behavior modification and is therefore extremely influential.

REINFORCEMENT IS THE MOST POWERFUL TOOL THE TEACHER CAN USE TO AFFECT BEHAVIOR.

This is a return to the basic fact that people are pleasure seekers. Behavior modification has simply taken that basic fact and devised strategies for arranging the environment to supply pleasure as reinforcement for specified behaviors. When students accomplish a previously stated educational objective, they should be justly paid (reinforced). In this plan, successful teaching is associated with the successful arrangement of the environment. The instructional design maximizes the environmental conditions which will provide the reinforcement to expedite the learning of specific objectives. In its implementation, students are given *reasons* for doing things.

Candy Is Dandy

It is sometimes illuminating to find out what can be used as a reinforcer. Some things are already known—people will generally work for praise, attention, a new car, a high grade, athletic achievement. For many children, a simple piece of candy is a very powerful motivator. Research studies of behavior modification have found M & M's to be a favorite. Promises of a few M & M's, or a couple of jellybeans, or a chocolate-covered cherry have been used to elicit remarkable behavioral changes in children (see especially Azrin and Lindsley 1956).

But reinforcement is more than the giving of a reward as an inducement for students to do something they may not otherwise do. In fact, it is not always the giving of a reward. A more specific term than reinforcement, reward means a positively valued factor—that is, something a person considers in a positive way, something worth having and worth working for. Reinforcement, however, can include factors generally interpreted as negative. For example, pain is a negative state of affairs, something people will not try to attain. People will therefore try to avoid it, and the avoidance of pain is a positive state. When you have a headache, an aspirin may reduce that headache. The aspirin thus becomes a reinforcer since it results in the avoidance of the aversive state.

Further, what may be reinforcing to one person in one situation may not be reinforcing to another person in the same situation, or to the same person in a different situation. Although winning an athletic contest is normally a rewarding, reinforcing event, it can actually be a terrifying experience to a dependent, overprotected athlete (Ogilvie and Tutko 1966). Most of us interpret winning as inherently pleasurable, often with accompanying cultural advantages. An insecure athlete may find, however, that by winning the dependency needs are reversed. Such a performer can no longer look to others, who instead will look to the winning athlete. Because of the winning, the individual's dependency on others has been taken away. As another example, it has been shown (Nuttin and Greenwald 1968) that verbal praise given a student who has completed particular academic endeavors is generally very meaningful when given by the regular teacher; but when given by a stranger, it loses its potential, even though the stranger uses exactly the same terminology.

It's Not What It Is: It's What It Does

A reinforcer can be anything a person is willing to work for. What it *is* does not matter; its effect is what counts. As an illustration, consider the following brief account of an interaction observed between a practice teacher and a seventh grade student in a physical education class.

> Andy was considered by most teachers a serious discipline problem. He initiated disruption in nearly every class, regardless of teacher or subject. Almost always he was given some form of punishment for his behavior, varying from an angry glance to verbal beratement and even physical infliction. Nothing seemed to work. In physical education class, the practice teacher's standard reaction to his disruption was to stop what she was doing and simply wait silently for Andy to "settle down." As time went on, she began to add verbalizations such as "The rest of the class is waiting for you to stop, Andy," or "Do you mind if we continue?" or even "Let me know when you're finished so we can go on."
>
> It was obvious that Andy, not the teacher, was in control of the class. The supervising teacher suggested that the attention given to Andy by the practice teacher was strengthening the disruptive behavior.

Can this be true? Of course it can. Attention is normally a very strong reinforcer. Even if the teacher had administered punishment for his disruptive behavior, Andy may have been willing to endure it for the reinforcement of the attention it afforded. His classmates, in fact, might also have added to the attention by giving social approval for the disruption, thus reinforcing the reinforcement itself. Although in many situations this may be true, in Andy's case it was not, for the class generally did not favor him as a person and disapproved of his meddlesome antics. Nevertheless, a psychological assessment indicated Andy's strong needs for attention which he was receiving in the physical education class. Graphically, the following was happening:

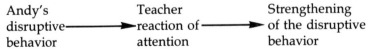

Andy's disruptive behavior ⟶ Teacher reaction of attention ⟶ Strengthening of the disruptive behavior

Since attention was the reinforcer, Andy discovered that by creating a disturbance he could receive attention; therefore the disruptive behavior was being reinforced and consequently was more likely to occur in the future.

To eliminate the disturbances, it was decided that a different reaction was necessary. The answer seems quite clear, but its execution is difficult.

The supervising physical education teacher and the practice teacher decided that what had to be done was to ignore Andy when he was mischievous and instead give him attention and praise when he was not disruptive. Previously, Andy had been ignored when he was not creating a disturbance.

At first it was perplexing and awkward. When Andy did not receive the usual attention for his annoyances, he began to increase the intensity of the disruptions, which made it particularly difficult. It appeared for a time that ignoring the disturbances was only going to increase their incidence. But suddenly, one day, Andy seemed to give up, seeing that he was not getting results. In the meantime, the practice teacher had made a concerted effort to give Andy attention for the times he was not causing an agitation, and often, following the class, she would spend a few moments in nonspecific conversation with him. He seemed especially to enjoy those times. Recognizing that, the teacher would talk to him only after class on the days when he had not created a disturbance for the entire period. Resultingly, in four weeks, Andy's discordant conduct almost disappeared.

We can see, then, a new cycle of events taking place:

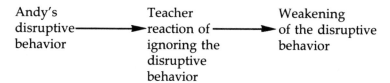

Andy's disruptive behavior → Teacher reaction of ignoring the disruptive behavior → Weakening of the disruptive behavior

Or we can look at it a different way:

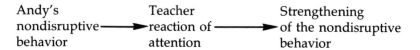

Andy's nondisruptive behavior → Teacher reaction of attention → Strengthening of the nondisruptive behavior

It is of course difficult (if not impossible) to completely ignore disruptive behavior at all times. Nonetheless, the principle of modifying behavior states that

- Any behavior which is reinforced will *increase* in frequency in the future.
- Any behavior which is ignored will *decrease* in frequency in the future.

In this regard, we can consider the two opposing behaviors in Andy's situation: disruptive and nondisruptive. Further, we can consider the disruptive behavior undesirable and the nondisruptive behavior desirable. Consequently, we are left with the conclusion that if desirable behavior is reinforced it will increase, and if undesirable behavior is left unreinforced it will eventually disappear. This procedure is often a large order. But thorny as it may be at first, it involves a predictable human response, based on the important behavioristic conviction that

NO BEHAVIOR WILL PERSIST IN THE ABSENCE OF REINFORCEMENT.

Whatever does not receive attention will eventually be gone. Andy's disorderly conduct, difficult to ignore, *must* nevertheless be ignored; and although it will take the patience of time, it will then go away. Furthermore, it will be replaced by the opposite behavior, nondisruption—Andy cannot be cooperative and uncooperative at the same time. So, if the nondisruptive times are reinforced and subsequently increase in frequency, they will simply replace the disruptive times.

Opposites Do Not Always Attract

To a great degree, then, behavior can be thought of in terms of opposites. One behavior supplants the other. A student cannot be simultaneously antagonistic and concurring, nor respectful and disrespectful, nor listening to the teacher and talking to other students.

Moreover, these behavioral opposites normally are also opposite in desirability. A teacher wants students to be on time for class, not to be late; or to participate in activities, not to avoid them; or to improve in motor performance, not to regress.

Thus, we can usually make a list of behaviors considered desirable and find opposites considered undesirable. For example, suppose a desirable behavior for a movement education class is for students to devise new ways of moving on a balance beam. Obviously the opposite is *not* devising new ways, which is something of a contradiction. But since the two are in opposition, if the plan of behavior modification is accurate, the teacher need only attend to the desired behaviors, while ignoring the others.

Desirable Behavior	Undesirable Behavior
Inventing new movement patterns on the balance beam	Using the same movement routines on the balance beam

Using this contraposition analogy, it is possible to devise a whole series of desirable behaviors, each of which may be paired with an opposing undesirable behavior. For example:

Desirable Behavior	Undesirable Behavior
1. Being on time for class	1. Not being on time for class

2. Dressed in appropriate attire for class	2. Not dressed in appropriate attire for class
3. Standing quietly for roll call	3. Being disruptive during roll call
4. Attending to the presentation of the lesson	4. Annoying others during the presentation of the lesson
5. Being involved in class activities	5. Showing avoidance of class activities
6. Working on class assignments	6. Ignoring class assignments
7. Handing in homework on time	7. Handing in homework late or not at all
8. Practicing specified movement skills	8. Performing movement skills haphazardly
9. Exploring new ways of doing movement skills	9. Repeating the same way of doing movement skills
10. Practicing movement skills independently	10. Annoying others while they are practicing movement skills
11. Cooperating with others	11. Exhibiting isolate behavior
12. Showing respect for others	12. Being inconsiderate of others
13. Increasing scores on fitness tests	13. Maintaining or decreasing scores on fitness tests
14. Improving movement skills	14. Maintaining or decreasing movement skills
15. Increasing knowledge of mechanics of movement skills	15. Failing to understand mechanics of movement skills

Always, any behavior that is included on the desirable side can be considered an objective. Whatever is listed, however, the important feature of such dichotomous pairings is that *only the desirable behaviors* receive the reinforcement. The undesirable behaviors should then disappear.

Doing Nothing, Forever, About Something

Suppose it's a cold day and when you try to start your car, nothing happens. You try again and the engine still does not start. You turn the key more firmly and the engine still refuses. Now you get angry and grind the key into the ignition. Does this help? Of course not. But it is a natural human reaction—when we do not obtain the normally expected results for our efforts, the immediate reaction is often to try the same behavior again, but with more feeling.

Think again of the situation with Andy. As long as his teacher was willing to ignore the undesirable behavior (the disruptions), the probability of its disappearance was increased. But if the teacher had given him a revival of the attention he was accustomed to receiving, everything would have returned to square one. Not only that, but the disruptions would probably have reached a new intensity by the time they were again reinforced. Why? Because when Andy no longer received the predictable response of attention from the teacher for his disruptions, his initial response would be to *increase* the intensity of the disorderly conduct in a more serious effort to get his payment. Just like turning the key harder in the ignition, Andy would try harder. Suppose the teacher, at some future time, reaches a saturation point with Andy's new effort at disruption and once again responds to his actions. What will Andy have learned? That he has to work a little harder for the attention. Consequently, the attention is now reinforcing the heightened disruptive performance, and a new pattern is evolving.

Originally, it was a matter of

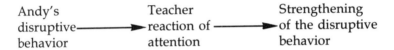

Then, the situation became changed to

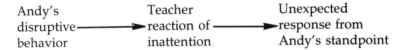

With the withdrawal of the expected response, Andy's immediate reaction may be

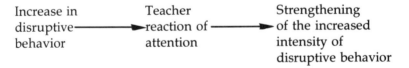

The cycle may be repeated, for Andy may learn that he has to increase the increase, in effect heightening the intensity of his disruptions each time to obtain the attention. Thus the actual *increase* in disruptions may also be reinforced. In different form, it looks like the following chart.

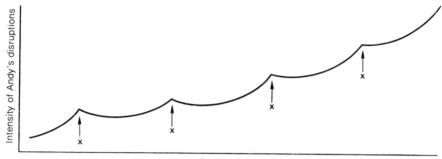

Factor of time
Each "x" represents the teacher giving attention.

Reinforcement will strengthen whatever behavior it follows. Therefore, if it occurs after any of Andy's new and intensified disruptive efforts, that reinforcement will set off a potential chain of events which will result in greater and greater increases in the discordant behavior. The moral:

WHEN REINFORCEMENT IS WITHDRAWN FROM A PARTICULAR BEHAVIOR IN THE ANTICIPATION THAT THE BEHAVIOR WILL SUBSEQUENTLY DISAPPEAR, SUCH REINFORCEMENT MUST BE COMPLETELY WiTHHELD UNTIL THE BEHAVIOR DOES IN FACT DISAPPEAR.

It's all or nothing. A slip here and there ruins the whole affair. Once a decision is made to take reinforcement away from an undesired behavior, that decision also requires the fortitude to see it through. It may be difficult at times, but it's an absolute necessity.

You Might Not Be Doing What You Think You Are Doing

The events happen daily, in classes everywhere, with students controlling and teachers unaware—an aversive class, a well-timed disruption, and a product of avoiding the aversive class. We probably all fall victim in some form, at some time.

The influencing force is not so much the attention given as *when* it is given. Here's a little exercise on timing. Suppose you are teaching a swimming class, and one of the established rules is no running on the deck. Of course there is no absolute obedience, although the violations generally occur during "free-swim" times. In such a situation, how would you answer the following questions?

1. What is the behavior you want (the desired behavior)?
2. What is the behavior you do not want (the undesired behavior)?
3. Which of these two behaviors is more likely to receive attention?
4. On the basis of reinforcement theory, which of the two behaviors is more likely to persist in the future?
5. What can you do to promote the desired behavior?

In this situation the running may be a spontaneous happening rather than an attempt to secure attention. If so, it may not increase in occurrence, but neither will it necessarily *decrease* unless it results in an undesirable state for the students involved—usually, some form of punishment. In contrast, some sort of trade-off may be worth a try. For example, when a free-swim period results in *no* running on the deck, the time of the next free-swim will be lengthened. The reward for no running is more free-swim time. The shortcoming in such an arrangement is that the entire class may be "punished" for the actions of a few. That still may be all right, for when a reinforcer is desired by the entire class (as free-swim time presumably is), it can be a powerful influence which exerts intragroup pressures on all members to perform the behaviors required for the reward (Axelrod 1977).

Positives Always Increase the Result

Any stimulus which maintains or increases a behavior has, in a broad sense, a *positive* influence on the person. For that reason, it is usually referred to as a *positive reinforcement*. The stimulus itself may be anything that results in such an effect.

> A POSITIVE REINFORCER IS ANY STIMULUS FOLLOWING A RESPONSE WHICH WHEN PRESENTED WILL RESULT IN AN INCREASE OR A MAINTENANCE OF THAT RESPONSE.

It isn't what the reinforcer is, but its effect on behavior which is important. The most important feature of the reinforcer is how it is viewed by the individual. To have a positive effect, the reinforcer must be something desired by that person.

> WHATEVER IS MEANINGFUL TO A PERSON CAN BE USED AS A REINFORCER FOR THAT PERSON.

In the true sense of behavioristic analogy, if it works, it is effective. Whatever reinforcer brings about the desired behavior, that reinforcer should be used. One simply needs to *observe* the effect of a particular reinforcer to decide whether or not it is working.

One precaution should be noted: the reinforcer must match the person. Whereas a gold star beside their names may be reinforcing to younger students who achieve particular goals, it may not be so valued in high school. Wearing different colored jerseys in accordance with scores attained on a fitness test may be reinforcing to some students, offensive to others. Grades themselves may be more reinforcing to some students than to others.

Stimuli can be divided into *primary* and *secondary* reinforcers. Primary reinforcers are those which someone is willing to work for directly—attention, prestige, and free time, for example. Even food has been used as a reward for eliciting certain motor behaviors (Meyerson, Kerr, and Michael 1967) and the learning of certain academic skills (Wheeler and Sulzer

1970). More often the reinforcers used to achieve desired behaviors are not in themselves the influential factors, rather they *represent* other satisfactions which can be obtained *through* them, in which case they are referred to as secondary reinforcers. Money is one example—people do not normally work just to have the money but for the possibilities it represents.

Glaser (1971) has itemized a complete series of secondary reinforcers which seem to have no logical connection to the stimulated behaviors they have produced, yet each has been successfully employed in behavior modification programs. They range from poker chips given retarded children to shrunken heads awarded in primitive tribes. The conclusion remains that *anything* can be used to produce desired behaviors.

A Token Economy

Secondary reinforcers are generally easier to use. A customary example is the awarding of certain "tokens" to children in exchange for achievement, with the understanding that these tokens may be turned in at a future time for some more desired type of reinforcement. For instance, the teacher may give gold stars to students who spell twenty words correctly. When each student accumulates five stars, fifteen minutes of free time will be given to read magazines, work puzzles, talk to someone else, or engage in some other desired activity (which is acceptable to the teacher). In physical education, a swimming teacher may award students a point for every length of the pool swum with a prescribed stroke and ten minutes of free swim for every ten points accumulated.

Descriptively, the following illustration of the token system has been used in a real occurrence:

> Carl introduced in his second grade physical education class a unit designed to assist ball handling skills. He organized the class into a series of "stations," each of which had task objectives. At one station, for example, students were to bounce a ball as many times as they could, at another they were to throw a ball at a target, and so forth. A rotation system was used whereby each student spent five minutes at one station, then moved on to the next, until all stations had been visited. Each day Carl awarded poker chips for certain performances or improvements over previous performances. He also made available a list of reinforcers which students could work for, including such things as helping to get the equipment ready, choosing the Friday activity (free-activity day), announcing the time for station rotation, helping to give out poker chips, free time to look at comic books, and being pushed on a rope seat by the teacher. Some reinforcers were "five-chip rewards," while others were ten, and so on. Each student kept a box with the accumulated chips which could be saved up for any reinforcer the child wished.

And in another actual example:

> Debbie had a small high school physical education class (seventeen students) which had requested not to participate in the upcoming gymnastics unit. The group wanted to play basketball instead. Debbie decided to use basketball as a reinforcer. An empty auxiliary gynasium was available during the class time, and Debbie arranged an agreement with her class whereby students could "buy" their way into the empty gym to play basketball. And

"buy" it was, literally, for Debbie used play money to pay students for performances in gymnastics. Certain accomplishments were worth more than others. Each piece of apparatus had a series of suggested tasks with a stated value, ranging from $.50 to $2.00 for each maneuver. To become eligible to play basketball in the free gym, every student had to accumulate $5.00 each day, earning the money through the gymnastic performances. Money could be saved from one day to the next.

Such examples are no different from the football coach who plasters the players' helmets with decals for outstanding performances. The reinforcers, not necessarily valuable in themselves, are used to elicit behaviors which are desirable.

Grandma Knew It a Long Time Ago

Looking back, Grandma really knew what she was doing. She said things such as:

"When you eat your potatoes, you can have some ice cream."

"After you take your bath, you can watch some television."

"If you clean up your room, then you can go out and play."

"If you get all your homework done this week, on Friday we'll take you to a movie."

"Keep your room clean this week, and you can have a friend sleep over this weekend."

"If you're quiet in church, I'll give you some candy."

She asked for a *specific* behavior before allowing you to have something you wanted. She knew that by giving access to something you desired, she could get you to do something you might not otherwise have done. With due respect, in behavioristic circles this principle is called "Grandma's Rule." In definitional terms:

ACCESS TO HIGH-FREQUENCY BEHAVIORS CAN SERVE AS REINFORCERS FOR THE PERFORMANCE OF LOW-FREQUENCY BEHAVIORS.

More formally called the *Premack Principle* after its originator (Premack 1959), in its simplest form, it says that all one needs to do is watch people and see what they like to do, and then use those things as reinforcers for their doing the things they might not normally do. In other words, use what people want to do to get them to do what *you* want them to do.

Carl did it. So did Debbie. They offered student-desired reinforcers in exchange for student performance of teacher-desired behaviors. The most appealing feature is that this method is based on a positive rather than negative foundation. Students know what they must *do*, not what they must *avoid*. There is no threat involved.

The Premack Principle is another statement in support of the basic premise that people will work to achieve satisfying states. To be totally effective, however, certain factors must be observed.

1. A valued reinforcer must be available. The reinforcer cannot be something the teacher *thinks* ought to be reinforcing; it must be something that has proven value to students. Usually this implies a wide selection of reinforcers from which students can choose. The only difficulty may be in first determining the available reinforcers. This issue may be settled directly: *find out* by observation and inquiry what students value. In other words, watch what they do in their free time in class, or simply ask them what they would like as reinforcers.
2. The reinforcer must be given only *after* the desired behavior has taken place. The low-probability behavior should occur first, followed by the high-probability reinforcer. Students must *earn* their rewards.

   There may, however, be certain exceptions. In some instances a reinforcer may be presented first. For example, if a basketball teacher has agreed with students that an occasional scrimmage will be given as a reward for hard work in practice sessions, a surprise scrimmage may be a catalyst for the following practice days. This is the basis of the American economy—a credit card for the pleasure before the pain. But failure to pay off the credit at a later time incurs a penalty. So it must be with students. If the class (or individual student) does not follow up with the retroactive earning of the privilege, there should be some form of penalty—if nothing more than the withholding of future reinforcements.
3. The reinforcement should be stated in positive terms. It is less effective to say,"If you don't practice these swimming skills this week, you can't have a free swim on Friday," than it is to say,"If you give an honest try to these swimming skills, you can have some free-swim time on Friday." This is a contrast to the presentation of threats as stimuli for performance. Thus it is working *for* reinforcement rather than trying to *avoid* punishment.
4. The reinforcement must be given as soon after the desired behavior as practical—in some cases immediately. Social reinforcement, for example, is most potent when given as soon as possible following a reinforceable behavior; its effectiveness tends to dissipate with time (Skinner 1969). In other cases, an unavoidable delay in the attainment of the reinforcer can actually be used to advantage, for there is evidence (Sulzer and Mayer 1972) that delayed reinforcement can result in greater persistence in the desired behavior than if the reinforcement were given immediately. That is, in fact, one of the features of the token system (the delay is a sort of "bridge" to keep interest high until the reinforcer can be earned).

Frugality of Credit

Reinforcement *can* be overused. Too generous a dose of any reinforcement may reduce its value. Praise, for example, will be viewed with suspicion if it is very easy to obtain or if it comes too abundantly.

The amount and quality of the reinforcement given should be directly related to the obvious nature of the individual's behavioral responses. Thus credit should be withheld when the causes of the behavior are obvious. For example, we do not ordinarily compliment someone for coughing, even though the result of the coughing is quite valuable. There is usually not much of an alternate choice for such behavior; therefore no credit is deserved. So it is with students. When they behave in desirable ways in the midst of great possibilities for exhibiting undesirable behaviors, they deserve more credit than when alternative possibilities are not available. In this regard, an atmosphere of threat reduces the students' deserving of credit because the threatening atmosphere itself removes many alternative behaviors. Reinforcement therefore should generally be given in inverse proportion to the conspicuousness of the causes of the behavior. There is no need to waste credit on behavior which is reflexive or near-reflexive in nature. Nor should reinforcement be given for what someone has done by accident. We can also withhold it when others will provide it anyhow, such as when students provide each other with reinforcement. These are matters of good management—for when students realize they must legitimately work for it, reinforcement will be received with more value when it is obtained.

A Lesson from One-Armed Bandits

Assume you are in Las Vegas standing in front of a slot machine. You drop in a quarter and nothing happens, just lemons. Another quarter, more lemons. Still another and another. After three dollars and seventy-five cents, you are ready to quit. But the machine won't let you, for just about that time it pays off. Then it will keep you there until it has its money back.

Slot machines are programmed. Their payoff is based on behavioristic principles. They are set to reinforce the gambler at the moment when most people are ready to quit. Their mechanical control comes from research which has determined how long the average person is willing to persist at a given task without receiving any reinforcement. These machines are telling us that teachers should do the same.

It's another lesson in the effective management of reinforcement: Use only as much reinforcement as necessary to elicit desired behaviors. Get as much for your money as you can, in effect.

Here's an illustration. A story is often told as an example of Zen (although a teaching principle is involved as well) about an archery instructor who was extremely successful through teaching by "nonteaching." Hypothetically, here is the response of one of his students:

> I was starting to get frustrated. I mean, we had spent two whole weeks just drawing the bow and not shooting an arrow. He kept talking about how we need to be in full control or our muscles before we could expect to hit our target. I was trying. My arms were still fighting me, however. And now my persistence was also. He'd come around to me and watch me draw the bow and say nothing. I mean *nothing*. More and more I tried to do what he was telling us. I was actually beginning to get the feeling he was talking

about—a sort of controlled relaxation. Then one day, as he stood next to me, I felt particularly at ease and in control at the same time. I looked at his face, and he smiled and nodded. Only later was I to realize how much that small gesture meant to me at the moment. (Adapted from Herrigel 1971)

Slot machines and Zen archery instructors both reinforce only at the moment when performance is ready to drop off. Both use only what is necessary to keep behavior going.

Very directly, the research (see especially Favell 1977) says that in the beginning stages of learning, reinforcement should be given often. Then, as behavior becomes stronger, its frequency should be decreased. The outcome is greater persistence in the selected behaviors, for students will work harder for the reinforcement they are accustomed to receiving.

Think back for a moment to the scenario with Andy. When he did not receive the usual attention for his disruptions, he tried harder. Then, in response to the increased intensity of disruptions, the teacher could either continue to withhold attention or to give it, in which case Andy would either drop his disruptions (if he received no further attention) or continue his augmented disturbances (if he received attention at the new intensity). We can now take that same arrangement and apply it to the *intentional promotion* of desired behaviors. It's a matter of purposely waiting until the desired behavior begins to show signs of fading and then providing the reinforcement to get it going again. A picture would look something like this:

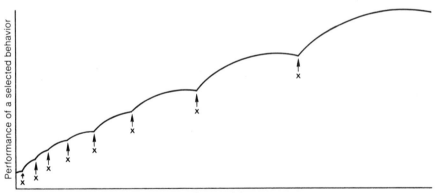

Factor of time
Each "x" represents the teacher giving reinforcement.

In the beginning, reinforcement is given often. Then it is progressively withheld, requiring students to work harder to obtain it. In this simple format, reinforcement finds its most effective employment.

CHAPTER 11

Starting New Behaviors

The discussion thus far has dealt with the means for dealing with behaviors already existing within the repertoire of individuals. The affairs of behaviorism could be considered complete at that, and sometimes they are. Even the classical function of education (to change behavior) is based on the supposition that the only behaviors needing alteration are those that students already have. The more ultimate objective of education, however, is to initiate *new* behaviors in students—those which are not already part of their total conduct—which isn't quite so easy.

Reinforcement theory specifically states that a behavior must first *occur* before it can be reinforced. But how, for example, can a parent reinforce language development in an infant who has never uttered the semblance of a word? Or how can a physical education teacher reinforce a seat drop on the trampoline until a student actually *does* it? Can a swimming teacher reinforce jumping off the high board for a child who has never jumped off the high board? Can a tennis teacher reinforce a topspin serve before it occurs?

What can be done? Must we wait until desired behaviors accidentally happen before we can reinforce them?

Accepting Near Misses

In a sense, new behaviors *can* originate out of existing behaviors. They can be, in effect, refinements of gross behavioral patterns. Thus a child's illegible scribbling becomes recognizable handwriting. Or a young bike rider learns to coordinate movements with the bike. Or a beginning golfer develops more control of the ball.

In behavioral terminology, this is called *response differentiation*. In theory it begins with the common technique of reinforcing desired behaviors while leaving others unattended. In practice, however, it spreads the reinforcement to include not only the desired behaviors, but also the *approximations* of those behaviors. It directly incorporates a wider range of potentially reinforceable behaviors. Simply stated, response differentiation gives credit for a near miss. Therefore,

TO INITIATE A NEW BEHAVIOR, IT IS USUALLY NECESSARY TO REINFORCE APPROXIMATIONS OF THAT BEHAVIOR.

Under this broader scope of behavior modification, what now qualifies for reinforcement is behavior which is roughly correct, similar to, or even related to, a goal. Parents wishing to reinforce their infant's attempts to say "mama" will naturally respond to approximations by smiling, repeating the word, or hugging so that the child will continue the attempts. The physical education teacher who wishes a student to learn a forward roll must first accept and reinforce any kind of legitimate approximation as evidence of the desired behavior.

The following real situation is given as a sample case of a teacher's use of response differentiation.

> Connie is a physical education teacher at an elementary school. One day her second grade group was joined by a withdrawn child named Marie whose parents had just moved to town. Every class day upon entering the gymnasium, Marie immediately went to a corner and sat down, refusing to participate in the activities. At first Connie tried to encourage Marie; then she tried some mild threats. Nothing worked. Then she decided to ignore Marie for awhile to see if it would have any effect. It did not.

> The desirable behavior was for Marie to become a fully participating member of the class. Because no approximation of that behavior was occurring, there was nothing to reinforce—until one day when Marie stood up, just stood up. Trite as it may seem, standing was better than sitting, for at some time standing was needed as a first effort to join the class. When she saw Marie standing, Connie went over to her and made some idle conversation and then told her some things the class would be doing next time. At the time of the next class, Marie went again to a corner. This time, however, she did *not* sit down but remained standing. Again Connie went over to tell her of the things the class was doing, never once suggesting that Marie should join. After about three days, Marie began to move out of the corner and to take up a position along the side of the gymnasium. Minor as it may seem, this was another approximation of the desired behavior. So Connie reinforced it. Then one day, in a sudden emancipation as she watched another student performing a ball-bouncing skill, Marie said to Connie, "I can do that." Connie's short response:"I'll bet you can." Marie made no further response; but at the close of that class period, as the other students were preparing to return to their rooms, there was Marie at the side of the gymnasium, bouncing a ball. "By golly, you're right," Connie said to her. "You do that really well. And I think you could probably do some of the other things the class is doing also."

It took several months before Marie became a fully participating class member. It *did* happen, however, as the result of the principle that

REINFORCEMENTS GIVEN TO APPROXIMATIONS OF A DESIRED BEHAVIOR USUALLY GENERATE CONTINUED PROGRESS TOWARD THAT BEHAVIOR.

There were times when Marie regressed to a previous behavioral pattern, but this is a fairly common occurrence in response differentiation. It is the same kind of situation as when we play the game where one person hides an object and then gives verbal cues to another trying to find it: "Cold." "No, you're freezing." "Now warm." "Getting warmer." "Hot!"

In a similar, documented case (Johnston, et al. 1966), a three-year-old boy's extremely low level of physical activity was changed to a normal level through the systematic application of social reinforcement. The boy was spending all his free time (at a preschool) in idle, solitary play in a sandbox, when his teachers decided on a target behavior of having him climb on a set of "monkey bars." To do so they first reinforced behavior which would get him out of the sandbox. Then they reinforced behaviors to move him closer to the bars and finally to touch the bars. At each stage, the teachers reinforced his approximations of moving toward the bars and then withheld further reinforcement until the boy made the next overt approximation. Finally, they reinforced him only when he made his first attempts at climbing the bars, withholding the ultimate reinforcements until he was actually climbing. At the end of the academic year, through this program, the boy's physical activity was considered perfectly normal in every respect.

Shaping Up

The process of generating new behaviors is usually referred to as *shaping*. Part of the technique includes response differentiation, but more specifically it refers to the actual application of systematic reinforcements.

SHAPING IS THE SYSTEMATIC REINFORCEMENT OF SUCCESSIVE APPROXI-MATIONS TOWARD A DESIRED BEHAVIOR.

Note the inclusion of the word *successive*. This means that to reach an objective, one must normally proceed in a series of stages rather than arriving instantaneously at the target behavior. Connie had to reinforce small overt progressions toward the end behavior of having Marie become a participating member of the class. The three-year-old boy needed reinforcement for every movement toward the initial objective of having him stand next to the climbing bars. Furthermore, as we shall see in the next few pages, the technique of shaping may be the most important aspect of the behavioristic method of teaching motor skills. It may also be one of the more difficult yet truly artful applications of behavior modification.

Getting There Is Half the Fun

In order to fit a true behavioristic format, a learning experience must be adaptable to the present performance level of each student. It must also provide each student with the same opportunity to attain relative success. Such a program can be designed and effectively applied in physical education. In its basic form, it can look something like the following:

Objectives of the
learning experience

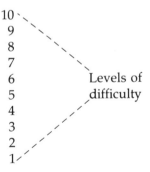

Each number represents a gradual increment in difficulty from a basic performance level (1) to an advanced performance level (10). As such, the numbers also represent a series of performance objectives arranged in successive order as a step-by-step outline of sequential learnings. In addition, they represent the content of teaching, as we shall soon see.

At the very top of this outline is an overall objective for the particular learning experience. For illustration, assume that this objective relates to students learning a tennis forehand. Then, supporting that objective are the ten levels of successive performances which are the steps toward efficient skill in the forehand (which will be discussed later).

Now, suppose you have a high school class of thirty students beginning a unit on tennis. Assume that twenty students have about the same present level of skill attainment. They are able to perform at, say, the fourth level of difficulty. Of the remaining ten students, assume that five can perform at the seventh level of difficulty and the remaining five are true beginners, able to execute only the first level of difficulty. Thus the "entering" ability levels for this class of thirty students are as follows:

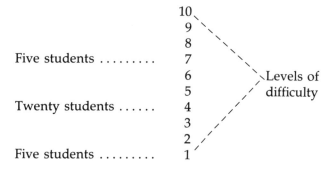

If it were assumed that all thirty students were ready to perform at the fourth level of difficulty and that the lessons for the *entire class* should begin at that level, then there would be a somewhat certain guarantee that five students would be bored and five others would be frustrated. Instead, the lessons must begin at the *present performance level for each student*. This means that at least three (and potentially thirty) programs will occur simultaneously.

This isn't as impossible a task as it may seem. It begins with the normally neglected operation of finding out exactly where each student is at the beginning of the learning experience. The progressive levels of performance have already been outlined, sometime before the unit began; thus the first event is to test or to observe all students in the class. In our hypothetical example, the testing has shown that twenty students do not need to attend to the first three levels of difficulty, five have already accomplished the first six levels, and five more are at the first level. So we have found out that certain steps can be *eliminated* for some students. The three programs therefore look like this:

Objectives	Objectives	Objectives
10	10	10
9	9	9
8	8	8
7	7	7
6	Five	6
5	students	5
4		4
Twenty		3
students		2
		1
		Five
		students

It is not necessary to compile a different learning sequence for each student; rather it becomes a matter of students starting at different levels in the *same* program. The variable is the number of *specific objectives* already accomplished by each student. Accordingly, the expectations also vary in relation to the present level of performance that each student brings to the learning situation. Thus the five students presently at level 1 would not be expected to get as close to level 10 as the students at level 7. If a student at level 1 advances to level 4, however, then that student deserves the same credit as one who starts at level 7 and makes it all the way to level 10. Therein is another advantage of this discrete system: it clearly illustrates what is normally called "improvement" and does so in such fashion that there is no doubt of the relative nature of the improvement.

Inside the Levels of Difficulty

The real science of this system begins even before it is put into use. The applicability and the validity of the technique are dependent on the *content* of the levels of difficulty. This means that each level must be described with the attention to detail characteristic of behaviorism.

At the very top of such a teaching strategy must be an overall objective—something considered an accomplished performance, even though it is recognized that the majority of students may not reach that final objective. The purpose of this overall objective is to give direction to the subgoals which are then listed as the progressive steps toward the overall end product—they are the levels of difficulty. In the previous illustration, the overall objective was to facilitate the learning of an effective forehand in tennis. This target behavior can be described as finishing in "the ability to hit a forehand, from behind one's own baseline, to land the ball within ten feet of the opposing baseline, varying the height and placement of the ball at will." Although the language used in such objectives can be relatively liberal, the successive levels of difficulty must be described in definite and observable terms.

The levels of difficulty are sort of rungs on a ladder, each one more accomplished than the preceding lower one. Thus in arranging a series of steps for a tennis forehand, we may come up with descriptions resembling the ten in the following list, starting with the most basic and progressing to the more difficult.

Level 1. The racket is held in the proper forehand grip.

Level 2. The entire body rotates into the backswing, arms remain relatively low, with elbows close to the body.

Level 3. At the moment of contact with the ball, the racket face is perpendicular to the intended line of flight of the ball.

Level 4. The weight shifts from the back foot toward the front foot during the foreswing, moving in the intended line of flight at the moment of contact with the ball.

Level 5. The racket head accelerates at the moment of contact with the ball.

Level 6. The ball is contacted off the "front surface" of the body, with the wrist in a laid-back position at the moment of contact.

Level 7. The speed of the racket head is adjusted relative to the intended force of the hit.

Level 8. Arm swing describes an inside-out plane in the foreswing.

Level 9. Body position is adjusted relative to the oncoming ball, allowing the player to execute as many of the preceding levels as often as possible, regardless of the position of the ball.

Level 10. The direction of the swing can be varied for intentional imparting of spin on the ball.

In describing these levels, each of which, in theory at least, is more difficult than the preceding, the list not only provides the behavioral objectives, it also presents the teaching plan.

Several recognitions automatically accompany the construction of such a list. First of all, the levels of difficulty must be stated in terms that students can understand, for they are involved with the performances. Students should be *shown* the list of objectives so that they may fully understand what is expected of them. If it becomes evident that students do not understand the content, the original wording may need alteration. The list of tennis objectives given is a brief illustration of how the levels of difficulty might be written for students. Level 2, for example, may need rewriting in some form such as the following:

As the ball approaches your forehand side, your entire body rotates as a unit, feet shifting as necessary. In this rotation your elbows stay as low as they were when you were in the ready stance, waiting for the ball, and both hands stay on the racket handle in the early part of the rotation. Then, as you reach the end of your rotation, the hitting hand alone takes the racket back another foot. At the end of this backswing, your racket should have been taken back no further than a half-circle away from the direction you want to hit the ball.

Even this description may leave some students puzzled, and one may eventually conclude that it is almost impossible to write descriptions of the levels of difficulty which will be received with the same meaning by *all* students. Therein lies the intrinsic value of a visual demonstration of the skills accompanied by verbal explanations. Further, the teacher can provide the *reasons* for the content of the objectives, such as in level 2 where the underlying factor is to *prevent* the very common tendency of beginning tennis players to lift the elbow to draw the racket into the backswing. Thus the description also complies with the behavioristic concept of informing students what to *do* instead of what *not* to do.

Another important consideration in writing such lists is that transitional steps may be needed between the levels. For example, a student may have difficulty in going from level 1 to level 2. The student is able to demonstrate the appropriate forehand grip (level 1), but becomes a bit entangled when attempting the backswing. Consequently, it is necessary to insert a step between the two levels, level 1a. Thus the teaching of a ready stance may facilitate the backswing. If not, sublevels 1b and 1c may need to be inserted until the desired behavior for the backswing is observed. The point is that each level of difficulty will have certain *supportive behaviors* which will assist students in making the jump from one level to the next; but to state all these behaviors would clutter the list, particularly when most students will perform them anyhow. Nonetheless, the teacher must know what the supportive behaviors are, keeping them in reserve and pulling them out when a particular student needs those sublevels in order to progress to the next stage of learning.

Furthermore, it must also be recognized that any list of levels of difficulty is subject to student individuality. While the original list may be constructed on the basis of *increasing difficulty*, in practice the levels may not necessarily represent increments in difficulty for *every* student. Hypothetically, the levels are supportive of each other—level 1 is prerequisite to level 2, level 2 is essential to level 3, and so forth. Some students, however, will have accomplished the upper levels without having achieved the lower ones. Therefore, the list of the levels of difficulty may in fact not be arranged in an increasing order of behavioral demands for all students. Still, the list is not invalid, for it represents a logical *teaching sequence*. Thus it serves not only as an outline of the behavioral objectives but also as a guide for the arrangement of the educational experiences.

The levels of difficulty also provide stages at which it becomes logical to offer students reinforcement. Each level is an achievement within itself. Advancing from one level to the next deserves recognition, whether going from 2 to 3 or from 9 to 10; and such advancement affords the teacher a series of checkpoints at which reinforcers may be made available to students. Included in this potential is the reinforcer of achieved grades, for reason has it that the student who advances from level 1 to level 4 may be just as deserving of a high grade as the student who advances from level 7 to level 10. However, this conclusion is predicated on the assumption that movement from one level to the next is always of equal difficulty. In reality, this may not always be true.

The final major factor to consider is that the step-by-step improvement in student learning is a matter of *performance*, not of time. In other words, the levels of difficulty are performance factors and do not demand that advancement be made with regard to certain time stipulations. Theoretically, no time factor should be involved. When a student moves from one level to the next, no matter how long it takes, it is the result of an ability— a success—rather than a product of imposed time demands.

Just the Facts; Nothing but the Facts

Now for the real substance of the matter. Behavior modification is only as good as its content. In the preceding example, if the levels of difficulty are illogically constructed, or if they contain unrealistic expectations, or if there are meaningless behavioral demands within the levels, then the list does not meet the behavioristic requirement of efficiency. Contrastingly, the levels of difficulty must contain only the *absolute essentials* to meet the overall objective of the learning unit. Therefore

THE LEVELS OF DIFFICULTY ARE STATEMENTS OF THE PERFORMANCES WHICH ARE ABSOLUTELY NECESSARY FOR THE EFFICIENT EXECUTION OF SPECIFIC MOTOR SKILLS.

These levels are, in effect, those behaviors that *all performers* must do in order to learn the skill well. Furthermore, they are the only performances necessary for efficient execution. Resultingly, they will *maximize* teaching effectiveness, for this list of performances cancels out any attention to unessential behaviors.

This is the most difficult aspect of a behavioristic approach to the teaching of motor skills. It plays on the teacher's specific knowledge of the mechanical essentials of any skill. For example, look again at the list of the ten levels of difficulty given for the tennis forehand. Notice that nothing is really said about footwork. Does that mean that footwork is unimportant and does not need teaching attention? Not really, for "footwork" is actually built into level 4, which describes the shift in body weight that accompanies the foreswing. The implication is that when level 4 is performed, the appropriate footwork will be included; thus *isolated* attention need not be given. Certain patterns of footwork may exist as sublevels, however, and with some students the teaching of footwork may assist the transition from level 3 to 4. But the assumption is that it is not necessary for *all* students. Furthermore, observation of the performances of top-level tennis players leads to the conclusion that footwork is so variable that an exact statement about it cannot be made. Footwork changes with each forehand and seems to be more related to the position of the ball than to any standard performance criterion. Consequently, it can be concluded that if the top players are *not* executing any stylized footwork, then footwork is *not* an absolute essential for top-level performance, and it therefore does not need specific teaching attention for novice players.

The advantage of such a critical appraisal of the specific motor skill being taught is that it *eliminates* needless attention to the teaching of nonessentials. It avoids teaching efforts based on lore, or on what are assumed to be the essentials for effective motor skill performance, which in some cases may hinder rather than help learning.

An excellent example is found in the study by Breen (1967). Using slow-motion films to analyze the swings of major league baseball players batting over .300 and comparing them with the swings of hitters under .300, his analysis showed five (and only five) factors to be common to the swings of the top hitters. Every top hitter was performing all five factors, while at least one factor was absent from the swings of the lower group. Thus the distinguishing feature of the two groups was their ability to perform what appeared to be five performance essentials. Now here's the interesting thing—footwork *was* important for successful performance, but not in the usual sense. It is generally believed that the foot placement in the stride of a baseball hitter should be variable, depending on the location of the ball. Breen's study showed this belief to be false, for one of the five factors common to all the top hitters was that their stride and foot placement were the *same* each time, regardless of the type of pitch or where the ball was thrown. It can therefore be stated that variable foot placement works *against* success in hitting, and yet every spring all over the country, swarms of baseball coaches and teachers of softball are telling their students to "Step into an outside pitch and away from an inside pitch."

The Art of the Science

Every motor skill has its own peculiar performance essentials. For some skills the list is quite extensive, for others it may be rather brief. For instance, in shooting a free throw in basketball, is it conceivable that the *only* performance requisite is to project the ball higher than the rim? Is that all someone *needs* to do? It seems illogical but when one observes professional basketball players, the differences are evident. Most of these players have a similar finger placement on the ball, or a certain alignment between the ball and the elbow, or a certain sequential movement pattern for projecting the ball, and so forth. But not all the players will do the same things; consequently one is left with the conclusion that some of the normally accepted performances considered essential for success in free-throw shooting may not be *absolutes* since professional players appear to do quite well without them. Instead, in constructing a list of the levels of difficulty for free-throw shooting, only those factors which can be evidenced in the performance of *every* demonstration of success qualify for inclusion.

Even here, we run into some problems. Suppose we observed and charted the swings of skilled golfers. We would find that they all perform a curious little idiosyncratic movement prior to the backswing called a "waggle." It's used as a preliminary movement to generate the feeling of timing for the swing. The confusing thing is that while *every* golfer may execute this movement, each one does it in a slightly *different* fashion. So how do we teach it? It warrants inclusion in the levels of difficulty, but it cannot be described specifically—a requirement of behaviorist theory.

First of all, there is room in the behavioristic scheme for relativity. In other words, within each particular motor performance certain skill essentials are "relatively more essential" than others. In golf, for example, certain elements clearly *are* absolutes, for they are determined by laws of physics. To hit a ball into straight flight requires that the club be brought into the ball in a fashion predestined by the physical principles of colliding masses. Nothing can change in that respect. But the "waggle," because it is used by every skilled golfer, must be accepted in a relative sense. It appears to be an absolute only in presence, not in the exact manner of execution. Therefore, it should be included in one of the levels of difficulty with perhaps an open-ended description.

Another relative matter is that of the time available for the teaching of a particular skill. Usually, curriculum demands are such that only limited time can be allotted to each particular learning unit. Thus it is even more imperative that the levels of difficulty include only the essentials of each skill being taught. It may be, however, that a specific skill has certain "relative absolutes" (such as the waggle in golf) which could legitimately be included in the lists of the levels of difficulty, but because of constraining time limits, these not-quite-so-absolute factors must be left out. Nevertheless they remain in reserve, to be inserted into the teaching plan when time permits or when a student successfully completes all the original objectives.

This brings us to the most relative matter of all. Because of the fact that all learning units normally have time limitations, the teacher who designs the unit must make decisions regarding which performance objectives do exist as absolutes. Sometimes such decisions are not so complicated, as, for example, if ten weeks are allowed for learning archery. If only five weeks are available for gymnastics, however, the decisions about performance objectives will involve more possibilities. It is a true test of the rationale of the teacher. Insight and observation are sometimes better than written words; that is, on some occasions the recommendations available in books and articles are contradictory to an individual's observation of accomplished performers. Consequently, the construction of a list of absolutes must accrue from perception—the teacher's ability to recognize the real essentials—and not from what other sources say is essential. If there is an absolute in the effective utilization of behaviorism for motor skill learning, it is that the substantive content of the levels of difficulty must be the performances which *are*, in fact, the absolutes.

Adding Up the Score

Behaviorism seems to make sense. It is based on the very defensible position of being able to show observable results. In the days of accountability and related movements, something as demonstrable as behaviorism suddenly becomes a very valid approach to education. Before making any final decisions, however, we must see the total picture.

CHAPTER 12

Concord Out of Discord

Normal/abnormal. Good/bad. Pass/fail. Up/down. Black/white. Stop/ go. Out/safe. Winner/loser. One but not the other—never both.

Many real-life situations contain events which are mutually exclusive of each other. We cannot go east and west simultaneously, or ride and walk, or serve and receive. When we have a choice, a decision is frequently made on the basis of which alternative is either more appealing or less aversive. These things seem quite obvious. But that's because these are situations in which the alternatives are restrictive. One option automatically excludes the other.

This is *not* the case, however, with humanism and behaviorism.

On the surface they do seem to be opposed, perhaps even exclusive. It may appear impossible to be in control of a class while at the same time allowing an atmosphere of freedom. No one can teach in a programmed manner while simultaneously promoting self-discovered learnings. It's not possible to be two people.

Or so it seems.

It's Not a One-Choice Option

There is undeniably an intrigue to both sides. Each appears to be well founded in creditable theory and fact. Both are supported by recognized educational authorities. Both seem to answer many questions about what teachers should really be doing (or not doing). Both contain definite guidelines about (1) how to arrange the educational setting, (2) how students should be behaving, (3) what performances are to be expected of students, (4) how those expectations can best be facilitated, and (5) how they can be evaluated. However, both sides also leave some questions unanswered. In the final analysis it can be concluded that neither side is perfect. Neither system should be accepted by the teacher or bequeathed to students as the only and exclusive methodological approach to education.

The debate between these two teaching schemes is not just an academic exercise. It affects people's lives—both teachers and students. If a teacher were to accept either system completely to the exclusion of the other, the teacher's conduct would be greatly influenced. The setting of goals, the means for attaining those goals, and the appraisal techniques to be used would be predetermined. Additionally, the manner in which the teacher overtly related to students, both in and out of class, would probably be determined. Such a nearsighted view would be seriously constricting instead of enlarging and would lead to a restricted awareness of the potential of education.

Logically, then,

BOTH HUMANISM AND BEHAVIORISM HAVE DECIDED ADVANTAGES FOR TEACHERS AND STUDENTS; THUS THE EDUCATIONAL ARRANGEMENT SHOULD COMBINE THE POSITIVE ASPECTS OF BOTH.

After a careful scrutiny of each side, what ultimately emerges is a functional state of dual utilization. It *is* possible to consider students in terms of their observable behaviors and also to regard them with respect to their consciousness. It *is* possible to see students as subjective beings in an objective world. People *are* both absolute and relative. Teaching *is* both exacting and permissive.

What needs to be decided is *not* which teaching scheme is best, but rather which is best in certain circumstances. It is *not* a question of *how* to be regulative or open, for those issues are well settled in theory and fact. The real question is *when* to be directive and *when* to be nonintervening. Using both systems is a matter of *timing* in their application, for there is a time to give freedom and a time to use control.

THE EDUCATIONAL APPLICATION OF HUMANISTIC AND BEHAVIORISTIC PRINCIPLES IN A COMBINED FORMAT IS A MATTER OF KNOWING WHEN TO USE EACH ONE. IN SOME SITUATIONS THE TEACHER NEEDS TO BE VERY, VERY CONTROLLED, AND IN OTHERS THE TEACHER NEEDS TO BE VERY, VERY OPEN.

The resolution of this timing rests on a multitude of factors. Clearly, not every situation calls for humanism or behaviorism in its extreme form. Instead, a combination of the two is normally most effective.

A Common Ground

Appealingly, both humanism and behaviorism have based their objectives on producing *success*, although with different means and ends. For the humanist, the criterion of success comes in the form of inner values: self-determined learning, aesthetic pleasures, creativity, and the like. Behaviorism exists more on the outside, with realistically established external goals and appropriate steps for their successful attainment. The common factor in both philosophies is the ultimate objective openly incorporated and promoted in the two techniques—*positive growth for students*. For that effort alone they deserve the plaudit of merit.

Furthermore, each system has based its educational methods on positives rather than negatives. Humanism says that the inner feelings generated through free-discovery experiences are manifested in heightened positive self-attitudes; behaviorism supports its technique on the foundation of positive reinforcement. In fact, both accentuate the positive.

Two Forms of Truth

If humanism and behaviorism were forced into a head-to-head evaluation on the single criterion of tangible substance, behaviorism would be declared the winner. Behaviorism is clearly founded on legitimate research, with volumes of precise data to support its affirmations. Yet humanism is no less a truth merely because it cannot brandish as much research. Rather, the lack of research is directly due to the fact that humanism has the scientific disadvantage of finding its meaning in concepts, feelings, perceptions, and other internal happenings which are less absolute and more elusive of measurement. To deny the existence of such values, however, simply because they are difficult to observe overtly is to deny the reality of consciousness.

The real powers of the mind are untouchable. They cannot be found somewhere in the dark recesses of the brain or excised and kept in a jar to collect dust in biology laboratories. Sure, we can easily name the parts of the brain and describe their basic functions, but where is the control for thought, the locus for common sense, creativity, coordination?

With more careful analysis, behaviorism, too, is not so scientific and lawful as it may first appear. The operation of its technique does not work for *all* persons, at *all* times, in *all* settings. For example, the generally influential reinforcer of attention may not be so positively received by an extremely reclusive student. Or a recess period may not be pleasurable for a student who is frequently subjected to abuse from other students.

In further defiance of the compartmentalization of these two formats, it can be argued that humanism is evolving into a behavioristic attitude. In an effort to reduce misinterpretation, humanism has taken to stating its philosophy with ever-increasing verbal precision. These attempts to discover and define more carefully the conditions which stimulate humanistic endeavors (creativity, for example) are actually behavioristic enactments. Maybe Socrates was right: "Nothing is permanent."

Three Concessions

To be rational about resolving the issues between the two sides, it is necessary first to grant three provisos which affect the *relative* rather than the *absolute* way people learn. These three conditional factors account for the individual variations that violate the inviolate laws that apply to everyone in general but to no one in particular. Said differently, whether humanists or behaviorists, people are and always will be people.

1. *Different physiological bases.* Everybody is biologically different. Some persons have more efficient nervous systems than others. Some seem to have a higher order of neuromuscular integration. Some have mechanically better muscle-bone attachments. Muscle fiber structure differs among all people, as does circulatory efficiency. The sinew and chemistry and molecular arrangement of each of us differs enough to make us vulnerable to ourselves. Some persons quite simply have parents who gave them a physiology which allows them to learn more quickly than others. Other persons literally get in their own way—not because they want to, but because of the functioning of their neural system. By virtue of our subjection to the capriciousness of organic determinants rather than biological computerization, we are in fact individuals, physiologically. There are

those who, with their refined inner telegraphic system of neural transmissions, can seemingly do anything. There are others who can seemingly do nothing. In between there are the great masses who are forever destined to be average—but not typical—and forever individualistic.

2. *Different cognitive bases.* If any facet of human behavior is subject to individual differences, it is the mental encoding process. The internal workings of the brain are so far removed from a complete understanding that it is impossible to conclude that all persons receive, interpret, and respond to stimuli in exactly the same fashion. To be sure, the chemical processes of the brain *are* relatively known, and the physiology of neural doings *is* understood, but thought and feeling and values are highly individual. Past experiences, selective attention (and inattention), personal preferences, and momentary psychological states all add to the variability of individual cognitive processing. Further, each person possesses different degrees of perceptual integrative ability. Fluid and crystallized intelligence varies. So does pure cognitive energy. Although the brain can be biologically deciphered, it still belongs to each of us personally.

3. *Different laws of learning.* If for no other reason than the fact of the first two diversifications, the laws affecting the acquisition of knowledge and skill are also subject to circumstantial variation. In an absolute sense, a "law" is something unmitigating, holding true in all instances. But the laws which apply to learning are averages based on probabilities, not on absolutes. What seems to work for *most* teachers in *most* situations provides the laws. Even behaviorists will admit as much. Laws are approximations, as close as anyone can come to reality in dealing with the inconsistency of human behavior. Although we are all regulatory in a great many respects and are therefore vulnerable to considerable predictability in responding to certain situations, we remain in charge of our own volition. Thus no matter how predictable and lawful we may be, individual exceptions remain. Consequently, teaching will continue to be influenced by the unconformity of individual responses.

Defining the Teaching Process

Perhaps the problem can be resolved by an examination of the teaching process itself. It is a not-too-difficult concession that any definition of the teaching act is essentially a behavioristic endeavor. The more one defines teaching, the more behavioristic it becomes. Any model of the teaching/learning phenomenon, then, must incorporate some behavioristic definitions. No matter which side of the fence one may be on, the following considerations are most important:

1. *The learner.* Any approach to teaching must consider the learner the first and foremost factor. Whether there are global goals such as self-reliance or creativity, or more isolated objectives such as specific skill development, the concerns must revolve around the welfare of the learner. In this regard, humanism and behaviorism are in absolute agreement, for both consider students their focal point.

103

2. *Educational objectives.* Although devoted humanists may find any attempt to specifically define the intentions of education somewhat opposed to their ideals, even the desired outcomes of free-discovery learning must at some time be stated. To be stated, they must be understood; to be understood, they must be specific; and to be specific, they must be definable. This adds up to an exact delineation of what is expected of the particular teaching format to be used. No matter how programmed or freedom-oriented the application of the objectives may be, the process must be given direction by a rather specific definition of objectives.

3. *Learning experiences.* Having defined the objectives, the next logical concern is to determine how to reach those objectives most feasibly. This is a matter of constructing the educational environment and experiences which will maximize the probabilities of achieving the stated goals. As long as there is an underlying organizational intent, the setting may be very regulated or very open.

4. *Individualization of the experiences.* Humanism and behaviorism both recognize that learners operate on different levels and at different paces. Consequently, an important facet of the educational setting is to arrange it in such a fashion that all learners may start at their current performance level and then progress toward the objectives at their own rate. Neither humanism nor behaviorism supports the traditional teaching technique of presenting an entire class with the same material, at the same level of difficulty, and with the same expectations for the time allowed in learning. In both formats individualization is possible and absolutely mandatory.

5. *Performance monitoring.* Although far easier in a behavioristic format, both teaching strategies demand that constant attention be given to the relative progress of students. This may involve behavioral analyses (tests, skill performances) or more open-ended empirical observations. In any case, some means of assessing student performance is necessary to determine if the educational arrangement is accomplishing the stated objectives. Without such evaluative methods, the four preceding considerations are meaningless.

In an overall perspective, humanism and behaviorism are not so far removed from each other as they may at first appear. Certain characteristics of each blend into an agreement on the important concerns of education. On those issues which appear hopelessly lost in disagreement, we find that each can offer a portion of the answer. Thus the effect is to make us aware not so much of the argument, but of the alternatives.

CHAPTER 13

Four Essential Steps

Having considered the most important general factors in analyzing the teaching/learning process, it now becomes necessary to attend to the procedures essential to the internal workings of the educational endeavor itself. Not surprisingly, the formal arrangement of an educational design must be predicated on components similar to those discussed in the previous section.

The following four progressional steps appear to be a universally accepted approach to the process of teaching. They are part of both humanistic and behavioristic arrangements; in fact they are primary to *any* teaching plan. They exemplify the first absolute for teaching success—orderliness. In essence, their overall message is that you must know where you are going, how you will get there, and whether or not you have made it.

One: Identifying the Target Behaviors

As everyone knows, the objectives of physical education are often stated in rather loosely defined terms. Recognizably, some of the cognitive aspects of a humanistic physical education program are difficult to put into words. Nonetheless, in the broadest sense of the term "behavior," observational evidences of the internal conditions of students are always available. Thus this initial step is not so much an argument as to whether or not a particular educational objective can be observed as it is an effort to carefully define the *evidences* of that objective.

In effect, the result is a statement which is both an identification of the objective and a means for its evaluation. If, for example, an objective for a volleyball class is for students to be able to play the ball without carrying it, then the statement of that objective also becomes the definition of the observable evidences of the anticipated learning and the means for evaluation.

This dual utility of definition/evaluation is reflected in the fact that objectives should always be stated in terms of what students should be like *after* the lesson, not *during* the lesson. Therefore, it is not functional to state such an objective as "to provide students with learning experiences in golf." This is merely a statement of what is going on *during* the sessions and says nothing about the *purpose* of the experiences. Furthermore, it stands as a normal expectation of a *method*, whether humanist or behaviorist or something else.

An additional consideration in stating purposes is that they must be expected to occur within the time allowance of instruction. For example, some activities in physical education are characteristically thought of as "lifetime sports"—golf, tennis, bowling, badminton, swimming, to name a few. In defining objectives for these activities, it is easy to outdistance the learning experiences with such far-reaching objectives as "to provide students with lifetime skill in tennis." Although the teacher sincerely believes this to be a reasonable purpose (and philosophically it may be), the possibility of observing its accomplishment is simply not realistic. It is more logical to consider the specific ways that a short-term experience in tennis can contribute to the more distant (but never stated) objective of a lifelong interest.

It is also necessary to caution against "being-aware"-type objectives. Any ambiguous objectives such as "comprehending the strategy of basketball play" are simply too broad and do not define the evidences of accomplishment. Thus the potential for evaluation is also seriously reduced. The key to the elimination of such ambiguity is to state the objectives in *operational* words—as *performances* which can be expected as student behaviors resulting from the learnings. Quite simply, these are definitions which make the observation of progress possible. Therefore the use of such words as "understands," "appreciates," or "respects" is automatically eliminated. These words do not readily communicate the same meaning from one person to another.

Accordingly, in keeping with this attempt to be operational, of the following objectives for a tennis class, none is acceptable as stated:

To develop an appreciation of tennis
To respect the rules of the game
To develop social attitudes toward the game and other players
To become an intelligent spectator of tennis.

As written, they are too difficult to evaluate, and therefore it may be impossible to design educational experiences which are presumed to generate their outcome.

Clear definition of *attainable* objectives is the most functional means of indicating to all involved the exact purpose of physical education. Such definition provides the most useful criteria for selecting content, for arranging the learning activities, and for deciding on the kind of teaching procedures to be used. It does, in fact, guide all other teaching activities.

This seems to point to a decisive victory for behaviorism since it clearly states that absolutely *nothing* can be accomplished without first defining the target behaviors which are the objectives of any educational endeavor. It must still be recognized, however, that many legitimate concerns of physical education, particularly those of a humanistic nature, are in fact difficult (and sometimes impossible) to define. Attempts at such definitions of purposes (Annarino 1970; Murphy 1970; Varnes 1970; Mohr 1971) often dig the verbal hole even deeper, without denying their reality. Humanistic ideals are not disqualified on the basis of definitional elusiveness. Rather, it is incumbent upon the humanistic teacher to consider the acceptable evidences of humanistic objectives more carefully.

This means that a behavioristic *attitude* toward the defining of objectives for any physical education experience is the most realistic approach. Such an attitude does not discard *any* objective; rather it demands that the objective be as specifically determined as possible, particularly as it relates to the student *performances* which will be accepted as indications of the learnings.

Two: Selecting the Educational Experiences

Having defined the objectives, the next step is to determine the experiences in physical education which are likely to attain the objectives. We begin with the foundational belief that the experiences of the learner constitute the real meaning of education. What the teacher does is important, but it is possible for two students in the same class with the same teacher to have different educational experiences. More significantly, student interactions with the environment are the determiners of learning.

In a general view, it can be concluded that many different kinds of experiences can accomplish the same objective—as long as they meet the criteria of effective learning. This means that the teacher may have a wide range of possibilities available in planning for educational experiences. It also means that the teacher should not be limited by strict adherence to one teaching arrangement. Indeed, it appears (see especially Hyman 1974 and Bennett 1976) that teachers who are more versatile in their approach to educational planning are more likely to accomplish their objectives.

Some educational experiences are relatively easy to determine. If, for example, an objective of a unit in basketball is to improve free-throw shooting ability, then obviously the answer is to provide for directed practice in that skill. Other objectives, however, may be more evasive of specific promotion. In certain instances it is possible that educational experiences *cannot* be arranged to facilitate particular objectives. As an illustration, an educational arrangement designed to promote the learning of social skills may in fact produce social interaction and nothing else. To proclaim that it facilitates a "skill," which is transferrable to other settings, and which is probably unassessable, may not be valid.

The problem, then, is to select those experiences likely to achieve objectives that can be considered realistically attainable. In some cases the objectives will lend themselves to behavioristic programming, in other instances to discovery-type learning. In *all* cases, one overriding factor must be part of the plan: the experiences should be *directly related* to the objectives. A behavioristic discipline is therefore required—to attend directly to the desired objectives and to establish an environment which reinforces the behaviors directly related to those objectives.

Three: Organizing the Educational Experiences

Closely related to their selection is the consideration of how the learning experiences can be organized into a coherent program. No supreme law of psychology dictates the organization of the experiences; it is a question of what seems to make sense in any given situation, with any given teacher and students. Even so, occasionally intuition may be the only guide. Always, however, there is flexibility.

It is possible to achieve behavioristic ends through humanistic means and vice versa. For instance, a discovery method may be particularly valuable in the beginning stages of teaching a new motor skill to inexperienced performers. With an initial period of time for exploration and experimentation, students may generate their own motivation and consequently may be more receptive to any programmed instruction which follows. For example, the teacher may introduce a unit in gymnastics to children by arranging equipment for a first experience of nothing more than exploration. To stimulate early interest, he/she may offer some open-ended suggestions such as the following:

- Move around, under, and over the apparatus in any way that you like.
- See if you can find different ways to move across the apparatus.
- What different parts of your body can you use to give you support while you are on the apparatus?

Later, the comments may become more specifically suggestive:
- Since your center of gravity changes during that maneuver, what can you now do with your arms to help maintain your balance?
- Can you use your shoulders in some way to help you in that turn?
- Does it seem that a change in the rhythm of that maneuver would give you the time you need to execute without rushing through it?

This, of course, is the technique of movement education. The standard format begins with an allowance for totally unstructured exploration and then progresses into guided problem solving, always providing students with the opportunity for self-discovered answers. In its purest form, however, movement education remains steadfast in the use of experimentation as the learning medium. Contrastingly, the teaching can evolve into a more programmed form by becoming more and more specific in assisting the learning objectives of the experiences. Accordingly, the conversation may then be as follows:

- This time, as you do the roll, tuck your knees as close to your chest as you can and see if it makes any change.
- Do you think you might need a pause for a support position between those two maneuvers to help them blend together?
- I see you're having some difficulty with that mount. Let me demonstrate a little something, and see if you think it may help.

The process of student self-discovery remains, but the teacher has made more specific suggestions for the learning which was intended in the first place.

Perhaps, in the best humanistic sense of student-centered education, any unit of instruction may be started by enlisting the help of students to formulate objectives and to decide on procedures. Following that group process, the instruction itself can be relatively programmed toward the agreed objectives. Or, if the unit begins with the experimentation which is the philosophy of movement education, it is conceivable that programming may never become formally used, since the students may be "discovering" answers to the problems (and also accomplishing the stated objectives) without much need for the external assistance of the teacher. When utilized, however, programming is not to be thought of in the isolated sense of presenting information, but as the skillful use of questioning and suggesting in an effort to channel students into the desired responses. It can be used in *any* learning. For example:

- Now that you know how the tennis ball should be spinning so as to arc downward in its flight, let's find out how we need to hit the ball in order to give it that kind of spin.

- Since you have discovered that a soccer ball can be most effectively passed for short distances by using the inside of your foot, can you now discover how to change your kick to make the ball travel a great distance?

- Now that you know the most efficient position on the bicycle for riding on level terrain, can you determine how that position should change when going up a steep hill?

In this fashion students are "discovering" the answers to problems which relate to the specific objectives of the teaching plan. The particular learning was always there, always part of the original set of objectives. All that has happened is that students have been subtly "programmed" into their own discoveries by the teacher's use of artful communication. The students *think* they have been self-monitored, when in fact they have been directed. The only real change needed in this procedure relates to the degree of suggestive direction given by the teacher to obtain the desired behaviors.

A further consideration may be that some students will discover that the most efficient way of learning is to be taught—they may come to *want* the teacher to help them through the frustration of *not* discovering the answers to open-ended problems. If experimentation is the *only* technique used, the inherent danger is that some students, left completely to themselves, may *never* arrive at the objectives. Consequently, the more "formal" teaching becomes a welcome addition to the learning experiences. In this respect, the regarded *value* of the teacher's assistance may have been increased, in much the same fashion as we receive clues to a problem in logic found in a magazine (before we turn to page 79 for the solution).

This whole affair can work the other way as well. It is possible to teach students systematically to discover answers independently. As an example, a unit on tennis may begin with a relatively programmed instruction in the essential phases of the forehand and the backhand. Then, at some appropriate time after the basics have been learned, the educational arrangement may evolve into experimentation with the learnings. The teacher may ask students to intentionally vary their grip, or the plane of their swing, or their transfer of weight—with the intent of discovering the effects of these changes. In other words, the lessons begin with the presentation of the known mechanical standards for the efficient performance of ground strokes, and when students have demonstrated a learning (at least to a degree) of these standards, the experiences are opened up to the self-discovered effects of variations from the basic techniques. In effect, the teacher "saves" some time in the beginning, for it may take longer than the available time for students to discover the efficient mechanics of ground strokes through experimentation. This is particularly true when there *is* a mechanically effective way of performing a skill. In such instances, the teacher must bring students to a certain performance standard as quickly as possible so that the following allowance for experimentation can have meaning. It is a philosophical deduction that there must first be a ground floor of known information before a variation can have any relevance. The variation can then be compared to what is known.

There is, in fact, a built-in guideline in motor skills which indicates whether they should be approached from an experimentive or a programmed standpoint. It will be discussed fully in the next chapter.

Four: Evaluating the Effect

Evaluation is a process of determining to what extent the educational experiences are accomplishing the objectives. While it may be understandably difficult to suggest all the possible schemes that may serve as teaching plans for fostering the learning objectives, the evaluative process for *any* plan is relatively uncomplicated.

It begins where students *were*. Without knowing where students were at the beginning of a learning unit, it is impossible to tell what changes have taken place throughout the unit. Hence evaluation involves at least two appraisals—one at the start of the unit, the other at a later time.

Behaviorism may appear to have another vote—it requires that any learning unit start by first determining the entering performance level of each student. When this is known, then progress above that level can be accurately demonstrated. It is simply a matter of comparing the entering student behavior with the behaviors acquired as a product of the learning experience. The difference is the learning.

Although this seems like a simple answer to evaluation, there is a precaution. In behavioristic analogy, the only learning which can be validated is that which can be directly observed and overtly measured. In other words, the student can be given credit for having learned something only when the student can *do* it. Learning cannot be *assumed* to have occurred if it is not openly *demonstrated*.

This opinion sounds logical—especially as it refers to the accepted standard definition of learning, which says that it is a change in behavior; and a behavior is, of course, anything that can be *observed* as an actual *performance*. Even if one agrees with this behavioristic interpretation, however, there is still the possibility of *accidental* performance. A student may do something by chance while being observed. Therefore a more accurate definition of learning may be that it is a *relatively permanent* change in behavior. Even that one is not satisfactory, however, for a behavioristic discipline would not accept the use of a word such as "relative," which has no real meaning. The important point to be made, then, is that learning can be considered legitimate only when it can be observed as a repeatable part of someone's behavioral repertoire. It cannot be a chance occurrence.

Perhaps an illustration may add some clarity. Suppose you were teaching a class in bowling, a skill relatively easy to observe. First of all, the performer needs to execute movements which are quite stylized. These movements need to be repeated each time, since the approach does not deviate markedly from ball to ball. The approach is relatively short in terms of the space and the time required. Consequently, the skill is openly available for mechanical analysis and overt evaluation. As a result, the techniques for the skillful performance of bowling are well known.

In the best behavioristic tradition, then, you devise a list of the important performance components which you plan to use as a basis for teaching. The list includes the factors which you believe are the *essentials* for efficient bowling, and they comprise both the objectives and the means for evaluation.

Assume that your list has fifteen items. On the first day of class you observe everyone performing, and you check off the behaviors on each person's list as you see them executed. There's Mary, for example. She's already doing twelve. Tom is doing ten. But Jill is able to perform only four, and Ray only two. After the first day you chart all the observed behaviors of each student, and as a result you have a tangible guide to use as a basis for helping each student. Then, at the next class meeting, your lesson plan is already partly predetermined. Your chart shows that Mary knows how to execute the pushaway, and so does Tom, so there's no need to teach that skill to either Mary or Tom. In fact, there is no need for a group lesson on the pushaway since some students in the class already know how to do it. Neither Jill nor Ray, however, can execute this behavior. Thus your checklist shows a need for some individual attention to the pushaway for them.

It's all very neat. Your list tells you exactly what to attend to with each student, and also what to ignore, since each student has already shown some performance abilities. As a result, you can spend some time with Mary, who, according to your checklist, is not getting the proper lift on the ball at the time of release. You explain it to her, perhaps demonstrate a few times, and in a short while she is able to execute a proper lift. Great—check that item off her list; the next time you can go on to something else. Then you give some time to Ray, who still has not learned the pushaway. After a few minutes with him, he picks up the technique and the rhythm of the maneuver, and he thus receives a corresponding check on his list. No need to attend to the lift for Mary or the pushaway for Ray anymore, since they obviously have now learned these movements as evidenced by their behaviors in performing them.

It's the same with all the other students. All are on paper, with their present levels of accomplishment right in front of you each day. This checklist offers a visual justification for all your teaching efforts, and it most certainly personalizes the instruction.

But wait—something is wrong. On the next class day, when teaching Mary one of the items her checklist has shown she is not performing, you notice that the beautiful lift she executed yesterday has disappeared. Didn't she learn it? Of course she did, because she *did* it. Can she have forgotten so soon? And look at Ray—sure enough, he is not doing the pushaway today although he did yesterday. What's going on here?

Probably it's not so much a matter of forgetting as of not learning. Performance and learning cannot always be considered synonymous. Behavior is not invariably a permanent thing. It varies as a function of many factors, one of which is time, and the time between one class and the next may be enough for behavior to revert to the original state.

So here you are, making checkmarks one day and erasing them the next. People learn and then forget, or learn and then unlearn. Whatever happens, the fact that it *does* happen should create a bit of caution for accepting a one-time performance as evidence of true learning. It would be convenient and behavioristic, but . . .

An even larger cloud in evaluation concerns the difficulty of appraising the achievement of *all* objectives. Some learnings are not easily appraised by standard means. The humanistic objectives related to the inner person may in fact be impossible to evaluate. Furthermore, the foundational philosophy of humanistic teaching is that evaluation is *not* so important a part of the learning scheme anyhow. At the very least, evaluation is not considered in the sense of any kind of *threat* to students or as a *comparative* factor which gauges student performances against some norm or against each other. In fact, from the humanistic viewpoint, the evaluative process is often considered best determined by the students themselves in self-appraisal. Certainly many objectives of humanistic learning do not have a right/wrong dichotomy, and some probably cannot be externally appraised. Instead, their meaning is entirely individual—within the value system of each person.

With due respect to the precision of the behavioristic technique, it must be recognized that some human behaviors are not readily evaluated. At the very least, evaluation plays a *less dominant* role in their learning; and in some cases, the environment must be intentionally nonevaluative. This means that unless the evaluative process closely parallels the educational objectives, it is not serving its function. Conclusively, then, if the educational objectives can be clearly defined, such definition provides the means for evaluation. In other cases, if the objectives cannot be so precisely delineated, the evaluative means are not automatically provided. However, such objectives are not necessarily disqualified. Rather, in these cases the evaluative process is not so critical a factor in the total picture.

CHAPTER 14

The Motor Is the Method

One of the major objectives of any physical education program is to promote the learning of motor skills. Both humanism and behaviorism can make valuable contributions to this end. Best of all, the issues here are not so philosophical. In fact, there is a convenient package into which both can fit and little argument about the logic involved. As they relate directly to the teaching of motor skills, humanism and behaviorism come closest to complementing each other.

We start with the classification of motor skills as either *open* or *closed*, a concept first stated by Poulton (1957), who originally used it to describe differences in the skill requirements of industrial occupations. As it applies to motor skills, a closed skill is one of high complexity, and an open skill is one of lower complexity. In a very broad perspective, the complexity of a skill refers to the degree of difficulty inherent in its execution. The more complex a skill, the more difficult to perform. Thus, to determine whether humanism or behaviorism may fit the teaching of a particular skill, only the degree of complexity of that skill must be established.

The Perplexity of Complexity

It isn't quite so easy, however. Just what is a highly complex skill? Gymnastics, maybe? For most persons, but not for all. How about golf? Perhaps, but enough 70s are shot every afternoon to keep us from saying golf is complex for everyone. Maybe riding a bicycle? Or walking on a railroad track? Or throwing darts at the local pub?

As a matter of fact, the fundamental consideration of skill complexity is *not* the degree of mastery a particular individual has of the skill; rather, it is the essential nature of the skill itself. Accordingly, it may be concluded that skills which require strength, endurance, speed, or power are normally uncomplicated in their execution and therefore rank on the low end of a complexity scale. Conversely, skills which require fine muscle control or high levels of coordination are normally considered complex skills.

Determining the complexity of a given skill can be a complex undertaking. Because we must always admit to the humanistic recognition that people are individuals, what is complex for one person is not for another. Moreover, what is complex for one person on one day may not be so complex for the same person on another day. Nevertheless, the fundamental criterion remains that a complex skill is one that requires the performer to execute fine, discrete, and precise movements. Contrastingly, skills of lower complexity are those often referred to as "gross" skills, because their successful execution does not demand the same precision of movement. Thus the *mechanical analysis* of the relative precision of the skill determines its complexity.

Clearly an example of a complex skill, golf requires any player to execute a series of very precise actions in order to accomplish effective performance. Any slight deviations in clubhead path will send the ball into the slices, dribbles, skulls, and hooks that are the daily standard rather than the exception on any course. We are all too keenly aware that the ball magnifies our smallest mistakes. In contrast, a football defensive line player can effectively perform the skills of the position by executing relatively unrefined movements. Success in this case does not require so finite a sequence of movements. When a golfer is a quarter-inch off-center in bringing the clubhead into the ball the result will be a drastic deviation in ball flight. When a football defensive line player is a quarter-inch off-center in contacting an opposing ball carrier, however, there will be no effect on the resulting performance.

This distinction does not imply, of course, that football players are less skilled individuals than golfers. It merely says that the physical demands of the two sports are different. In fact, *all* motor skills can be categorized on the basis of the degree of precise movements required for execution. Oxendine has offered a brief example (1970, p. 29):

#5 (low complexity)	football blocking and tackling performance on the Rogers' PFI test running (220 yards to 440 yards) sit up, push up, or bent arm hang weight lifting
#4	running long jump running very short and long races shot putt swimming races wrestling and judo
#3	basketball skills boxing high jumping most gymnastic skills soccer skills
#4	baseball pitchers and batters fancy dives fencing football quarterback tennis
#5 (high complexity)	archery and bowling basketball free throw field goal kicking golf putting and short irons skating figure 8's

The interesting feature of this effort is that it reminds us that a particular sport is not a singular thing. Within what we characteristically think of as a distinct sport are various phases of the totality, either with different individuals performing different functions or with the same individual performing different activities. For example, notice on the chart that basketball appears at two places, which illustrates the fact that there are two distinct aspects of the game—one where there is free-flowing motion and another where the game is halted for the more static execution of a free throw. Similarly, football blocking and tackling rank as low-complexity skills, while the demands of the quarterback rank as relatively complex skills, and field goal kicking gets an even higher mark for complexity.

The implications for humanism and behaviorism: The categorical complexity of the particular skill greatly influences the teaching methodology.

The Qualities of Open and Closed Skills

Open and closed skills are considered to have several qualities which add to their total picture. Thus a closed skill is not only one of high complexity; it is also one which is performed in a *static environment*. This means that no objects are in motion prior to the skill execution and the environment is also motionless. For instance, when a golfer prepares to hit, no ongoing changes are occurring in the playing conditions, and no other players are in motion. Furthermore, there is no time factor, for the environment is perfectly content to await the golfer's swing. Accordingly, closed skills are also considered *self-paced*; that is, the performer can initiate the activity at will, without regard to any changing environmental conditions or time demands. The same is true of bowling. The pins will remain ready, waiting patiently for the bowler to impose a fourteen-pound ball on them. In the same way, the target does not move for an archer; nor the environment for a discus thrower; nor the water for a diver. All these skills are performed in a stable environment and are self-paced in execution.

Contrastingly, open skills are generally performed in a *changing environment*. An object, or the environment, or other players, or the performer, or all of them are in motion during the execution of the skill. Soccer is an example. The ball itself is in motion; when the ball hits a rut in the field of play, the environment affects the action. And twenty-two players are in constant movement, resulting in a continual change in the performance demands. Consequently, such skills are additionally considered *externally paced*, since the environment forces the performer into responsive and immediate action, and changes the requirements from moment to moment.

Accordingly, the attention of the performer is determined by the nature of the skill being executed. In a closed skill the environment is not doing anything, and there is no need to devote much attention to it. You can hit a golf ball whenever you're ready to do so, and in preparation you can concentrate on the actual mechanics of the skill you know you are about to perform. In the flow of a soccer match, however, or a basketball game, or a field hockey match, the attention of performers must be given to the ever-changing events of the environment. In these sports the performers must be "open" to a variability in skill execution.

These factors can be summarized in the following chart:

Closed Skills	Open Skills
High complexity	Low complexity
Self-paced	Externally paced
Performed in stable environment	Performed in changing environment
Performer's attention on mechanics of execution	Performer's attention on variability of execution

Therein is the significance for humanism and behaviorism.

A Predetermined Lesson Plan

Humanism has always promoted individuality and variability and adaptability—all of which are critical to the performance of an open skill. Behaviorism has always promoted precision and attention to detail and certainty—all of which are critical to the performance of a closed skill.

Let's consider this a little more carefully. The answer is not as unequivocal as it may seem, but there are undeniable relationships between open skills and humanism, and closed skills and behaviorism.

Think first of that classic example of a closed skill—golf. Because it is self-paced, executed in a stable environment, and highly complex, effective performance in golf requires a mechanically efficient and repeatable swing. Not surprisingly, the effective performance techniques are known, because golf has been thoroughly analyzed over the years. Accordingly, since the technique for effective play in golf is already *known*, student learning experiences can be easily arranged into the "levels of difficulty" described earlier. Furthermore, the content of each level can be readily defined in specific behavioral objectives.

Looked at from the standpoint of effective teaching, it is only logical to conclude that golf, or any other closed skill, is best taught by a scheme which is administered in logical step-by-step order. If an open-ended experimentive approach were used for a closed skill, the end product of student experimentations would be the same anyhow. In other words, the objective in a closed skill is not to produce individualism and variability so much as it is to learn *exact* ways of performing. This *must* be the intended effect of the learning experiences when a closed skill is involved, because the laws of physics say so. No variable performances are possible in golf—at least in the *absolutes*. The performances which must be executed are predetermined by physics. And behaviorism says that these absolutes are *everything* the teacher needs to be primarily concerned about.

Thus the answer for a closed skill is to approach it with a behavioristic attitude. *Telling* and *showing* students how to perform is a time-saving endeavor of effective management. Perhaps after students reach a certain performance level, some experimentation with the swing may be introduced; but until they learn the absolutes of golf, such experimenting will have less meaning.

On the other hand, an open skill does not demand so confined a ritual of exacting performance. The fluid nature of basketball play, for example, provides opportunity for considerable variability in individual performances. The mechanics are not so stylized or static. Since basketball play, or any other open skill, requires a response to the changing environment, the players who *can* be versatile will be successful. It is entirely logical, then, to conclude that a humanistic attitude—one of experimentive problem solving as the learning medium—is the reasonable way to arrange these educational experiences. Open skills require adaptability, and humanism facilitates it. Thus the movement freedom of the humanistic approach is an asset, for there is no need for all students to arrive at the same end of mechanical performances. Rather, there can be an acceptance of any technique which accomplishes the objective.

Somewhat conclusively, then,

CLOSED SKILLS ARE BEST TAUGHT WITH A BEHAVIORISTIC ATTITUDE, WHEREAS OPEN SKILLS ARE BEST FACILITATED THROUGH A HUMANISTIC APPROACH.

This statement does not imply one approach to the exclusion of the other. It is simply a guideline for the arrangement of the learning environment. Further, it offers implications about the use of reinforcement.

The Means or the End

Reinforcement is not exclusively a behavioristic technique. No teaching scheme, regardless of how open it may be, would ever deny the potential of reinforcement for promoting learning. As it is used in teaching motor skills, however, there is a difference in its direction.

Behaviorism reinforces the specifically defined approximations toward overt behavioral objectives. Humanism is more concerned with promoting variations on themes. In a closed skill, the actual physical *performance* is critical; while in an open skill the *result* of performance is important. In other words, a closed skill operates on the principle that if the performance itself is mechanically efficient, then the result of that performance will also be effective. In an open skill, however, the performance does not matter so long as it achieves the end result. Accordingly, in the learning stages the student attends to the mechanics of skill execution in a closed sport and to the product of the performance in an open skill. This difference also foretells the use of reinforcement. With a closed skill reinforcement should be directed at the overt motor approximations of efficient performance; with an open skill reinforcement should be directed at the results of any acceptable execution.

Said differently:

IN A CLOSED SKILL THE TEACHER SHOULD REINFORCE HOW TO DO IT; IN AN
OPEN SKILL THE TEACHER SHOULD REINFORCE GETTING IT DONE.

One says technique, the other says results. On the basis that it increases the behavior attended to and decreases behaviors not attended to, reinforcement of a closed skill resultingly increases the precision of execution; whereas reinforcement of an open skill increases versatility of performance.

A Partly Cloudy Affair

It must of course be recognized that all skills are not clearly open or closed. There are many shades of gray in between. Golf may be definitely on the closed end of the scale and football tackling on the open end, but the great majority of sports have elements of both. A baseball swing may seem like a closed skill, but because a ball is in motion adaptability is also required. Tennis may seem like a sport that requires a great deal of precision, yet both a ball and another player are constantly changing the environmental demands. Wrestling may seem like an open skill, yet the initiation of offensive maneuvers must be considered to have closed qualities.

Moreover, it must also be recognized that most open sports have closed elements. Although the game is played in an open setting, the football quarterback must execute skills which are essentially closed. The baseball pitcher performs a self-paced, mostly closed skill, while the fielders must be prepared with externally paced responses. A basketball game is a flowing, changing, open sport; but the game stops periodically for foul shooting, which is a closed skill. Likewise a field hockey game, a soccer match, or other open sport is frequently halted for the execution of more specific closed performances.

Furthermore, the learning of an open skill often occurs in relatively closed fashion. Dribbling a basketball in a game is an open affair, but the *learning* of that skill had to have some closed quality, for there are certain mechanically efficient ways of doing it.

Such factors lead to caution against making blanket evaluations of the relative complexity of sports skills. What must be considered instead are the individual requirements within the sport, and the environment which will best facilitate the learning of those requirements. Therefore it seems that the groundwork of skill learning for any sport should occur in a closed setting, while the application of many of those skills should then take on open qualities. In effect, the attitude of behaviorism provides the beginning stages—clearly defining the objectives and determining the steps for arriving at those objectives. Then, as skill learning progresses, the attitude of humanism can provide the adaptability required by many skills in the real performance of competition.

Attending to the Desirables

Behaviorism proposes that the teacher give attention to desirable behaviors and ignore the undesirable. This proposal is not denied by humanism. Certainly both methods wish to promote desired behaviors.

To this end, suppose you observed the following happenings among students in a class learning tennis backhand:

1. Weight on the back foot at the moment of contact with the ball
2. Use of the backhand grip
3. An accelerating racket head at the moment of contact with the ball
4. Weight on the front foot at the moment of contact with the ball
5. Initiating the foreswing with the elbow
6. A decelerating racket head at the moment of contact with the ball
7. Initiating the foreswing with the shoulder
8. Use of the forehand grip

Some of these behaviors are effective contributors to the backhand, and others are not. They may be easily divided into desirable and undesirable categories. Such an either/or list results in the following division:

Desirable Behaviors

2. Use of the backhand grip
3. Accelerating racket head at contact
4. Weight on front foot at contact
7. Initiating the foreswing with the shoulder

Undesirable Behaviors

1. Weight on back foot at contact
5. Initiating the foreswing with the elbow
6. Decelerating racket head at contact
8. Use of the forehand grip

These categories of behaviors are incompatible with each other. A player cannot use the backhand and forehand grips simultaneously. Behavior 3, accelerating the racket head at contact, is opposite to 6, a decelerating racket head. Behavior 1 is incompatible with 4, and 5 with 7.

Macht (1975) has named them "behavioral pairs," indicating that such combinations always consist of one desirable and one undesirable behavior, opposite and exclusive of each other, one of which should be reinforced and the other ignored. Unfortunately, in the real setting, it is often easier to call student attention to the undesirable behaviors rather than to the desirables. Some research (Patterson and Gullion 1968; Siedentop and Rife 1975) shows that physical education teachers give more verbal attention to undesirable than to desirable behaviors.

There is no disagreement between humanism and behaviorism in the attempt to promote desirable outcomes. Both focus on the positive. In teaching motor skills, this means giving primary attention and reinforcement to the essential mechanics of successful execution. This is not just a behavioristic technique—it is simply an effective promotion of learning.

CHAPTER 15

Selected Short Subjects

In almost any debate, the final resolution comes from an arbitration of both sides. This is also the case with humanism and behaviorism. Furthermore, since both have certain common features, they jointly answer some very real concerns in physical education. Some of these concerns have already been discussed; others are presented here.

A Disciplined Affair

One of society's oldest techniques for controlling behavior is the use of punishment. If we do not pay our bills on time, we must pay a penalty. If we are caught speeding, we receive a ticket. Actually, we *do* learn from punishment. We learn to pay our bills on time and to avoid speeding; as well as not to touch a hot stove or not to talk out in class.

Sometimes included in behavior modification programs, punishment can be a stronger influence on human behavior than positive reinforcement (Stedman, Patton, and Walton 1973); however, for the most part, it tells people what *not* to do and creates behaviors which *avoid* the penalties. It generates within people a sort of automatic goodness, but even in that are certain benefits. In an educational setting, however, the aversive conditions created by punishment may have some undesirable side effects.

Punishment may be an immediate answer to a discipline problem, and it may seem to settle an issue quickly and forever; but some punished behavior may reappear later, after the withdrawal of the punitive situation. Thus a student might displace punished behavior by directing aggression toward things that cannot fight back, such as physical objects (Wilson 1971). Or there may be complete submission and a heightened state of fear (Hart 1968). One of the strangest potential outcomes is that of increased student aggressions on each other (Wheeler and Caggiula 1966).

While punishment may be a convenient response to a disruption, alternative ways of educational housekeeping are nevertheless more effective in the long run. One strategy is to reduce the opportunity for the occurrence of punishable behavior in the first place. Humanism contends this is best accomplished by eliminating many standard managerial acts so common in physical education, such as strict arrangements for roll call, inspection of uniforms, explanations of rules, and so forth. It must also be cautioned that a reduction in such regimentation will likely result in an initial *increase* in student disruptions, and only with time will students recognize that the new freedom is actually beneficial to them. Thus, although the incidence of disruptions may at first increase, later they will drop off to a lower level than under the strict managerial atmosphere (Chamberlin 1971). This finding supports the humanistic technique of giving freedom to students in gradually increasing amounts rather than suddenly discarding all regulations. Relinquishing managerial tasks also allows the teacher more time to interact with *individual* students to facilitate *individual* learning in whichever method is most appropriate.

If you are a humanist, you probably believe that all students will behave in civil ways unless they have a reason not to do so. Such a belief is part of the innate goodness which humanism automatically bestows on students. But it is also easy to misinterpret freedom as being synonymous with random permissiveness. There *are* certain advantages in being permissive—it may eliminate the need of supervision, and it normally does not generate the student counterattack which sometimes occurs in a restrictive atmosphere. *Total* permissiveness, however, is an illusionary arrangement and does *not* seem to work (Hearn, Burdin, and Katz 1972). Students must know that some behaviors cannot be tolerated, no matter how freedom-oriented the setting may be. Further, there must be a recognition that if these unacceptable behaviors occur, they will result in an aversive circumstance. A major factor is what constitutes the aversive circumstance. Rather than outright punishment, such a circumstance may be the *removal* of a positive reinforcer. Thus the teacher can respond to inappropriate behavior by *taking away* something that the student desires. Called *negative reinforcement* in behavioristic terms, this response acts to promote certain behaviors on the basis that a failure to perform them results in the withdrawal of a positive state. Such an event can thus be viewed as a negative occurrence. The "threat" imposed on students, however, is far more humanistic, for the "punishment" involved is the *loss* of a positive reinforcer rather than the *administration* of some sort of standard punishment. Further, this technique appears to be a workable alternative to the use of any threatened infliction (Skinner 1977).

The use of negative reinforcement does, however, place a demand on the teacher to construct programs which enable students to work *for* positive reinforcers. In the analogy described by Macht (1975), these positive reinforcers should be incompatible with the undesired behaviors. This means that positive reinforcers should be available for students who perform behaviors which are the *opposite* of those considered disruptive. In contrast, the classic approach to discipline problems has been to attend to the problems only *after* they have occurred. Probably the reason is because it's easy to forget to reinforce behavior which is considered appropriate; resultingly there is no recognition for being "good." It *does* take effort to respond to desirable behavior, but it can be accomplished by such small reinforcement contributions as merely saying to a student, "Don, you haven't pinched anyone else for two whole days. That's great!" or "Helen, you haven't been late for class all week. That's super!" Reinforcements can also include a more planned outline of "rewards" available to students who display cooperative behavior. Such techniques have proven value in reducing disruptive behavior (Boe and Church 1968; Brown 1971; Glaser 1971; McGinnies and Ferster 1971; Gilbert and Millenson 1972).

In situations where disruptive behavior does persist, even in the presence of such arrangements, behaviorism offers an outline of the procedure which can be used to eliminate the undesirable occurrences.

1. Specifically identify the behavior considered undesirable.
2. Identify the reinforcers which are maintaining that behavior.
3. Eliminate those reinforcers.
4. Make similar or equally valuable reinforcers available for the performance of the desirable behavior.

These suggestions are, of course, easy to say and much more difficult to do. Here's an example of how the procedure may be used:

> David had a habit of stealing sports equipment from the physical education lockers. Always he revealed the stolen equipment to his friends, who in turn supplied him with a perverse hero worship.
>
> Whenever something was missing from the equipment room and David was suspected of stealing by the physical education teacher, he and his locker were searched. David, who had hidden his cache in the meantime, reacted to the searching with verbal protests about an invasion of privacy, his innocence, etc., while his friends gave him further hero worship.
>
> A chain was in motion. David stole, he was searched, and he attained hero worship. The chain needed to be broken if the stealing were to be stopped. The physical education teacher therefore withdrew the searching, assuming that omitting it would stop the stealing since the hero worship occurred along with the searching. This technique did not work because hero worship was still available to David without the searching link in the chain. Thus it became apparent that the hero worship was maintaining the stealing rather than vice versa.
>
> A competing set of behaviors was needed. It just happened that David was quite skilled in swimming. The swimming coach agreed to make David a special project by giving him extra attention in swimming classes and ultimately inviting him to try out for the team. David did so, after much hesitation, and his performance was such that he became a team member. At this point, his teammates (with some encouragement from the coach) made an extra effort to provide David with a feeling of being an important member of the team. The result was a complete cessation of the stealing behavior, for a new route had been developed for David's need for attention.

The preceding incident happened. It illustrates the fundamental principle of reinforcing desirable behaviors. Specifically, research indicates (Campbell and Church 1969; Pai 1973) that the most effective plan is to reinforce those behaviors directly opposed to the undesirable actions.

Cautions About Creations

The methodology of humanism purports to foster spontaneous, expressive, and creative outcomes. Students are believed to develop inventive abilities through programs of self-discovered learnings. But a more cautious position must recognize the void in the available research supporting this contention.

This is a complicated matter, beginning with the fact that there is no universally accepted definition of creativity. The confusion is multiplied by frequently mistaking spontaneous behavior for creativity. Nonetheless, there *is* some evidence that certain forms of creative thinking can be stimulated through educational experiences which are specifically designed for that purpose (Eberle 1969; Schmidt, Goforth, and Drew 1975; Larsen 1976). Furthermore, there are enough references to lead one to the conclusion that creativity can be facilitated through a motor medium (Rugg 1963; Massialas and Zevin 1967; Feldhusen and Hobson 1972; Lieberman 1977). The real difficulty, however, is the very elusive nature of creativity.

In spite of the vagueness of the concept, one trait appears with a great deal of consistency in studies of creativity. Generally called *divergent thinking*, this trait refers to the individual's ability to initiate a variety of ways of looking at the same situation, and it appears to be a strong prerequisite to the development of whatever one considers creativity (Feldhusen, Treffinger, and Elias 1970). Divergent thinking, moreover, is a quality which can be independently facilitated (Taylor 1972; Luthe 1976; Scandura 1977).

Thus, while the research shows trends toward acceptance of the belief that creativity can be stimulated, the question then becomes how to promote it. A critical matter in educational environments is the requirement that the teacher provide for and stimulate student experimentations. Furthermore, during this time there must not be any evaluation of the resulting behaviors (Torrance and Myers 1972). For a humanist this is not a difficult stance to take; it is, in fact, a normal function of the philosophy. But a behaviorist may have a methodological block to such a position. Pure behaviorism cannot tolerate the uncertainty of something which is first of all indefinable and then is nonevaluated.

A conclusion to this dilemma may require behaviorism simply to make a concession. Not everything which exists in the world must have proof of its existence, and not every human ability needs absolute definition. While the research may be somewhat inconclusive, there is nevertheless a foundational collection (see especially Arieti 1976) which indicates that creativity, no matter how one defines it, *does* exist and *can* be facilitated through the problem-solving approach promoted by humanism.

The Monaural World Becomes Stereo

Properly given, an education is an adjustment between real life and the growing preparation for it. In a sense, it is making people fit company for themselves. It is a massive responsibility.

Physical education exists as a multidimensional avenue for the total development of all students. That's better than any book—better than television. In fact, physical education provides experiences which probably cannot otherwise be acquired.

Humanism and behaviorism provide physical education with concepts designed to increase the effective learnings of students. Both teaching formats offer new ways of looking at people; both are supremely concerned with enlisting positive outcomes. Behaviorism sees the reality of central issues; humanism says those issues lie inside people. Together they offer process and product.

If teaching is a science, behaviorism quantifies that science. If teaching is an art, humanism holds the brush. Yet the application of the science of behaviorism is a true art, and the timing in the use of humanism is actually a science. One is the artful use of a science—the other a scientific application of an art. Whatever it is, it isn't just one, but both.

References

Annarino, Anthony A. "The Five Traditional Objectives of Physical Education." *JOHPER* 41, no. 6, (June 1970): 24–25.

Arieti, Silvano. *Creativity, the Magic Synthesis.* New York: Basic Books, 1976.

Aspy, David N., and Roebuck, Flora N. *Kids Don't Learn from People They Don't Like.* Amherst, Mass.: Resource Development Press, 1977.

Astin, Alexander. *Four Critical Years.* New York: Jossey-Bass, 1977.

Axelrod, Saul. *Behavior Modification for the Classroom Teacher.* New York: McGraw-Hill, 1977.

Azrin, Nathan H., and Lindsley, Ogden R. "The Reinforcement of Cooperation Between Children." *Journal of Abnormal Psychology* 52 (1956): 101–102.

Bennett, Neville. *Teaching Styles and Pupil Progress.* Cambridge, Mass.: Harvard University Press, 1976.

Boe, Erling E., and Church, Russell M., eds. *Punishment: Issues and Experiments.* New York: Appleton-Century-Crofts, 1968.

Borton, Terry. *Reach, Touch, and Teach.* New York: McGraw-Hill, 1970.

Breen, James L. "What Makes a Good Hitter?" *JOHPER* 38, no. 4 (April 1967): 36–39.

Broudy, Harry S., and Palmer, John R. *Exemplars of Teaching Method.* Chicago: Rand McNally and Co., 1965.

Brown, Barbara. *Stress and the Art of Biofeedback.* New York: Harper and Row, 1977.

Brown, Duane. *Changing Student Behavior: A New Approach to Discipline.* Dubuque, Iowa: William C. Brown Co. Publishers, 1971.

Campbell, Byron A., and Church, Russell M. *Punishment and Aversive Behavior.* New York: Appleton-Century-Crofts, 1969.

Chamberlin, Leslie J. *Effective Instruction Through Dynamic Discipline.* Columbus, Ohio: Charles E. Merrill Publishing Co., 1971.

Cole, Henry P. *Process Education: The New Direction for Elementary-Secondary Schools.* Englewood Cliffs, N.J.: Educational Technology Publications, 1972.

Denzin, Norman K. "Child's Play and the Construction of Social Order." *Quest,* Monograph 26 (Summer 1976): 48–55.

Dreeben, Robert. "The School as a Workplace." In *Second Handbook of Research on Teaching,* edited by Robert M. Travers. Chicago: Rand McNally and Co., 1973.

Dunkin, M. J., and Biddle, B. J. *The Study of Teaching.* New York: Holt, Rinehart and Winston, 1974.

Durant, Will, and Durant, Ariel. *The Lessons of History.* New York: Simon and Schuster, 1968.

Eberle, Robert. "Experimentation in the Teaching of Creative Thinking Processes." *Journal of Creative Behavior* 3 (Summer 1969): 219.

Ellis, Michael J. *Why People Play.* Englewood Cliffs, N.J.: Prentice-Hall, 1973.

Erickson, Audrey. "Assessment of Readiness for Teaching." *JOHPER* 46, no. 3 (March 1975): 41–43.

Favell, Judith E. *The Power of Positive Reinforcement.* Springfield, Ill.: Charles C. Thomas, 1977.

Feldhusen, John F., and Hobson, Sandrak. "Freedom and Play: Catalysts for Creativity." *Elementary School Journal* 73, no. 3 (December 1972): 48.

————; Treffinger, D. J.; and Elias, R. M. "Prediction of Academic Achievement with Divergent and Convergent Thinking and Personality Variables." *Psychology in the Schools* 7 (1970): 46–52.

Field, Frank L. *Freedom and Control in Education and Society.* New York: Thomas Y. Crowell Co., 1970.

Fromm, Eric. *The Heart of Man.* New York: Harper and Row, 1964.

Gage, Nathaniel L. *Handbook of Research on Teaching.* Chicago: Rand McNally and Co., 1963.

Gensemer, Robert E. "Relationship of Fluid and Crystallized Intelligence to Ski Success." Paper presented at National Convention of AAHPER, Anaheim, Calif., 1974.

Gibran, Kahlil. *The Prophet.* New York: Alfred A. Knopf, 1965.

Gilbert, R. M. and Millenson, J. R., eds. *Reinforcement.* New York: Academic Press, 1972.

Glaser, R., and Cooley, William W. "Instrumentation for Teaching and Instructional Management." In *Second Handbook of Research on Teaching,* edited by Robert M. Travers. Chicago: Rand McNally and Co., 1973.

Glaser, Robert. *The Nature of Reinforcement.* New York: Academic Press, 1971.

Gowan, John Curtis. *Development of the Creative Individual.* San Diego: Robert R. Knapp, 1972.

Hammill, Donald D., and Bartel, Nettie R. *Teaching Children with Learning and Behavior Problems.* Lewisburg, Pa.: Allyn and Bacon, 1978.

Hart, H. L. A. *Punishment and Responsibility.* Oxford University Press, 1968.

Hart, Joseph T. *New Directions in Client-Centered Therapy.* Boston: Houghton Mifflin Co., 1970.

Havelock, R. G. *Planning for Innovation Through Dissemination and Utilization of Knowledge.* Ann Arbor, Mich.: Institute for Social Research, University of Michigan, 1969.

Hearn, D. Dwain; Burdin, Joel; and Katz, Lilian; eds. *Current Research and Perspectives in Open Education.* Washington, D.C.: American Association of Elementary-Kindergarten-Nursery Educators, 1972.

Hebbelinck, Marcel, and Ross, William D. "Body Type and Performance." In *Fitness, Health, and Work Capacity: International Standards for Assessment,* edited by Leonard A. Larson. New York: Macmillan, 1974.

Hendry, L. B. "A Comparative Analysis of Student Characteristics." Master's thesis, University of Leicester (England), 1970. Reported in *Personality and Performance in Physical Education and Sport,* edited by H. T. A. Whiting, et al. London: Henry Klimpton Publishers, 1973.

————. "An Exploratory Study of Expectations for the Physical Education Teacher's Role." Master's thesis, University of Bradford (England), 1973. Reported in *Personality and Performance in Physical Education and Sport,* edited by H. T. A. Whiting, et al. London: Henry Klimpton Publishers, 1973.

Herrigel, Eugen. *Zen in the Art of Archery.* New York: Random House, 1971.

Horn, John L., and Cattell, Raymond B. "Refinement and Test of the Theory of Fluid and Crystallized Intelligence." *Journal of Educational Psychology* 57 (1966): 253–70.

Hyman, Ronald T. *Ways of Teaching.* 2d ed. Philadelphia: J. B. Lippincott Co., 1974.

Jacobson, Edmund. *You Must Relax.* New York: McGraw-Hill, 1962.

Johnston, Margaret K. C.; Kelley, Susan; Harris, Florence R.; and Wolf, Montrose M. "An Application of Reinforcement Principles to Development of Motor Skills of a Young Child." *Child Development* 37 (1966): 379–87.

Jones, Tudor Powell. *Creative Learning in Perspective.* New York: John Wiley and Sons, 1972.

Kenyon, Gerald S. "Certain Psychosocial and Cultural Characteristics Unique to Prospective Teachers of Physical Education." *Research Quarterly*, March 1, 1965.

Kleiber, Douglas A. "Playing to Learn." *Quest*, Monograph 26 (Summer 1976): 68–74.

Klein, Roger D.; Hapkiewicz, Walter G.; and Roden, Aubrey H., eds. *Behavior Modification in Educational Settings.* Springfield, Ill.: Charles C. Thomas, 1973.

Kozol, Jonathan, *Free Schools.* Boston: Houghton Mifflin Co., 1972.

Laban, Rudolph. *Modern Educational Dance.* London: MacDonald and Evans, 1948.

———, and Lawrence, F. C. *Effort.* London: MacDonald and Evans, 1947.

Larsen, Gary. "The Effects of Different Teaching Styles on Creativity." *Journal of Creative Behavior* 10 (3rd Quarter 1976): 220.

Lengyel, Cornel. *The Creative Self.* Paris: Mouton, 1971.

Leonard, George. *The Ultimate Athlete.* New York: Viking Press, 1975.

Leukel, Francis P. *Essentials of Physiological Psychology.* St. Louis: C. V. Mosby Co., 1978.

Lieberman, Nina J. *Playfulness: Its Relationship to Imagination and Creativity.* New York: Academic Press, 1977.

Lortie, Dan C. *Schoolteacher: A Sociological Study:* Chicago: University of Chicago Press, 1975.

Luthe, Wolfgang. *Creativity Mobilization Technique.* New York: Grune and Stratton, 1976.

Lytton, Hugh. *Creativity and Education.* New York: Schocken Books, 1972.

MacDonald, W. Scott, and Tanabe, Gilfred. *Focus on Classroom Behavior.* Springfield, Ill.: Charles C. Thomas, 1973.

Macht, Joel. *Teacher-Teachim: The Toughest Game in Town.* New York: John Wiley and Sons, 1975.

Maltzman, I. "On the Training of Originality." *Psychological Review* 67 (1960): 229–42.

Marteniuk, Ronald G. *Information Processing in Motor Skills.* New York: Holt, Rinehart and Winston, 1976.

Martindale, Colin. "What Makes Creative People Different." *Psychology Today* 9, no. 2 (July 1975): 44–50.

Maslow, Abraham H. *Motivation and Personality.* 2d ed. New York: Harper and Row, 1970.

Massialas, Byron G., and Zevin, Jack. *Creative Encounters in the Classroom.* New York: John Wiley and Sons, 1967.

Merrill, M. David, and Tennyson, Robert D. *Teaching Concepts: An Instructional Design Guide.* Englewood Cliffs, N. J.: Educational Technology Publications, 1977.

Meyerson, L.; Kerr, N.; and Michael, J. L. "Behavior Modification in Rehabilitation." In *Child Development: Readings in Experimental Analysis*, edited by S. W. Bijou and D. M. Baer. New York: Appleton-Century-Crofts, 1967.

McGinnies, Elliott, and Ferster, C. B. *The Reinforcement of Social Behavior.* Boston: Houghton Mifflin Co., 1971.

Mohr, Dorothy R. "Identifying the Body of Knowledge." *JOHPER* 42, no. 1 (January 1971): 23–24.

Morris, Desmond. *The Human Zoo*. New York: McGraw-Hill Book Co., 1969.

Mosston, Muska. *Teaching Physical Education*. Columbus, Ohio: Charles E. Merrill Publishing Co., 1966.

Murphy, Betty Lou, "The Proper Focus of Our Field Is the Study of Sport." *JOHPER*. 41, no. 6 (June 1970): 27.

Newell, Allen, and Simon, Herbert. *Human Problem Solving*. Englewood Cliffs, N. J.: Prentice-Hall, 1972.

Nuttin, Joseph, and Greenwald, Anthony G. *Reward and Punishment in Human Learning*. New York: Academic Press, 1968.

Ogilvie, Bruce, and Tutko, Thomas. *Problem Athletes and How to Handle Them*. London: Pelham Books, 1966.

Oxendine, Joseph B. "Emotional Arousal and Motor Performance." *Quest*, Monograph 13 (January 1970): 23–32.

Pai, Young. *Teaching, Learning, and the Mind*. Boston: Houghton Mifflin Co., 1973.

Patterson, Gerald R., and Gullion, M. Elizabeth. *Living with Children*. Champaign, Ill.: Research Press, 1968.

Poulton, E. C. "On Prediction in Skilled Movements," *Psychological Bulletin 54* (1957): 467–78.

Premack, David."Toward Empirical Behavior Laws: 1. Positive Reinforcement." *Psychological Review 66* (1959): 219–33.

Pullias, Earl V. *A Teacher Is Many Things*. Bloomington: Indiana University Press, 1977.

Raths, James; Pancella, John R.; and Van Ness, James S.; eds. *Studying Teaching*. Englewood Cliffs, N. J.: Prentice-Hall, 1971.

Rice, Berkeley, and Cramer, James. "Comes the Counterrevolution." *Psychology Today*. 11, no. 4 (September 1977): 56–59.

Rickards, Tudor. *Problem Solving Through Creative Analysis*. New York: Halsted Press, 1974.

Roberts, Thomas B., ed. *Four Psychologies Applied to Education: Freudian, Behavioral, Humanistic, Transpersonal*. New York: Halsted Press, 1975.

Rogers, Carl. *Freedom to Learn: A View of What Education Might Become*. Columbus, Ohio: Charles E. Merrill Publishing Co., 1969.

Rugg, Harold. *Imagination: An Inquiry into the Sources and Conditions That Stimulate Creativity*. New York: Harper and Row, 1963.

Scandura, Joseph M. *Problem Solving: A Structural Process Approach with Instructional Implications*. New York: Academic Press, 1977.

Schmidt, Toni; Goforth, Elissa; and Drew, Kathy. "Creative Dramatics and Creativity: An Experimental Study." *Educational Theatre Journal* 27, no. 1 (March 1975): 111–14.

Schmuck, Richard; Chesler, Mark; and Lippitt, Ronald. *Problem Solving to Improve Classroom Learning*. Chicago: Science Research Associates, 1966.

Schroder, Harold M.; Karlins, Marvin; and Phares, Jacqueline O. *Education for Freedom*. New York, John Wiley and Sons, 1973.

Siedentop, Daryl, and Rife, Frank. "Behavioral Management Skills for Physical Education Teachers." In *Proceedings of the 78th Annual Meeting of the National College Physical Education Association for Men* (1975); pp. 167–74.

Singer, Robert N. *Motor Learning and Human Performance*. New York: Macmillan, 1975.

Skinner, B. F. "Between Freedom and Despotism." *Psychology Today* 11, no. 4 (September 1977): 80–91.

———. *Contingencies of Reinforcement*. New York: Appleton-Century-Crofts, 1969.

———. *Cumulative Record*. New York: Appleton-Century-Crofts, 1959.

———. *The Technology of Teaching*. New York: Appleton-Century-Crofts, 1968.

———. "The Design of Cultures." In *Control of Human Behavior, Volume 1: Expanding the Behavioral Laboratory*, edited by Roger Ulrich, Thomas Stachnik, John Mabry. Glenview, Ill.: Scott, Foresman, and Co., 1966.

———. "What Is the Experimental Analysis of Behavior?" *Journal of the Experimental Analysis of Behavior* 9 (May 1966): 213–18.

Smith, M. Daniel. *Educational Psychology and Its Classroom Applications*. Boston: Allyn and Bacon, 1975.

Spodek, Bernard, and Walberg, Herbert J. *Studies in Open Education*. New York: Agathon Press, 1975.

Stedman, James M.; Patton, William F.; and Walton, Kay F. *Clinical Studies in Behavior Therapy with Children, Adolescents, and Their Families*. Springfield, Ill.: Charles C. Thomas, 1973.

Stein, Morris I. *Stimulating Creativity, Volume 2: Group Procedures*. New York: Academic Press, 1975.

Sulzer, Beth, and Mayer, G. Roy. *Behavior Modification Procedures for School Personnel*. New York: Holt, Rinehart and Winston, 1972.

Taylor, Calvin W., ed. *Climate for Creativity*. New York: Pergamon Press, 1972.

Torrance, E. P., and Myers, R. E. *Creative Learning and Teaching*. New York: Dodd, Mead, 1972.

Travers, Robert M., ed. *Second Handbook of Research on Teaching*. Chicago: Rand McNally and Co., 1973.

Tschudin, Ruth. "The Secrets of A-Plus Teaching." *Instructor* 88, no. 2 (September 1978): 66–74.

Varnes, Paul R. "Physical Education Should Help the Child to Enhance His 'Physical Me' Concept—It Should Prepare the High School Student for His Physical & Recreational Adult Life." *JOHPER* 41, no. 6 (June 1970): 26.

Verhave, Thomas. "Recent Developments in the Experimental Analysis of Behavior." In *Control of Human Behavior, Volume 1: Expanding the Behavioral Laboratory*, edited by Roger Ulrich, Thomas Stachnik, John Mabry. Glenview, Ill.: Scott, Foresman and Co., 1966.

Wade, M. G. "Method and Analysis in the Study of Children's Play Behavior." *Quest*, Monograph 26 (Summer 1976): 17–25.

Walberg, Herbert J. "Changes in the Self-Concept During Teacher Training." *Psychology in the Schools* 4 (January 1967): 14–21.

Watson, J. B. and Rayner, R. "Conditioned Emotional Reaction." *Journal of Experimental Psychology* 3 (1920): 1–14.

Wheeler, A., and Sulzer, B. "Operant Training and Generalization of a Verbal Response Form in a Speech Deficient Child." *Journal of Applied Behavioral Analysis* 3 (1970): 139–47.

Wheeler, L., and Caggiula, A. A. "The Contagion of Aggression." *Journal of Experimental Social Psychology* 2 (1966): 1–10.

Williams, Robert L., and Long, James D. *Toward a Self-Managed Life Style*. Boston: Houghton Mifflin Co., 1975.

Wilson, P. S. *Interest and Discipline in Education*. London: Routledge and Kegan Paul, 1971.

Wolfgang, Charles H. "Teaching Preschool Children to Play." *Quest*, Monograph 26 (Summer 1976): 117–27.